Write Tight

Write Tight

▼

How to Keep Your Prose Sharp, Focused and Concise

▲

William Brohaugh

Writer's Digest Books

Cincinnati, Ohio

Write Tight.
Copyright © 1993 by William Brohaugh. Printed and bound in the United States of America. All rights reserved. No part of this book may be reproduced in any form or by any electronic or mechanical means including information storage and retrieval systems without permission in writing from the publisher, except by a reviewer, who may quote brief passages in a review. Published by Writer's Digest Books, an imprint of F&W Publications, Inc., 1507 Dana Avenue, Cincinnati, Ohio 45207. 1-800-289-0963. Portions of *Storycrafting* by Paul Darcy Boles, © 1984 by Dorothy Flory Boles, and reprinted by permission of Dorothy Flory Boles. First edition.

This hardcover edition of *Write Tight* features a "self-jacket" that eliminates the need for a separate dust jacket. It provides sturdy protection for your book while it saves paper, trees and energy.

97 96 95 94 93   5 4 3 2 1

Library of Congress Cataloging in Publication Data

Brohaugh, William.
    Write tight : how to keep your prose sharp, focused, and concise / by William Brohaugh.—1st ed.
        p.   cm.
    Includes bibliographical references and index.
    ISBN 0-89879-548-6
    1. Authorship.   I. Title.
PN151.B78   1993
808'.02—dc20   92-42070
                                                                                                        CIP

Edited by Jack Heffron
Interior designed by Brian Roeth
Cover designed by Paul Neff

About the Author

William Brohaugh has been editorial director of Writer's Digest Books since 1990. He joined the staff of *Writer's Digest* magazine in 1979, and became the editor of the magazine and its associated yearbooks in 1982.

His book work includes writing *Professional Etiquette for Writers*, and editing *Just Open a Vein*. He has edited *Writer's Market, Songwriter's Market* and *Photographer's Market*.

His published and produced short work includes more than 700 magazine and newspaper articles, magazine columns, short stories, children's plays, and radio and TV comedy scripts, and for even more fun he's dabbled in creating the occasional puzzle, trivia quiz and restaurant menu.

He would go on, but this book explains that one shouldn't write about things no one cares about, and he's already too guilty of that in these few paragraphs.

Dedication

*F*or Catherine, also writer and editor. Though ours is a mixed marriage (she ascribes to the *Chicago Manual of Style*, I to the *AP Stylebook*), it is one brought together and strengthened by hyphens (and by our discussions revolving around their necessity).

Table of Contents

Introduction
A Tight Fit Into Today's World

*W*hether you're writing paragraph-long anecdotes or sagas running to the thousands of pages, precision and concision of your words — what we will call writing tight — is crucial to the impact of your manuscript.

The need for tight writing has little to do with the frequently heard whine about how little time our readers have for us poor communicators these days, how short attention spans have become, how our words compete against the synchronized bowling match on ESPN and the war of the cartoon armadillos in the latest Nintendo game. ESPN wasn't around to distract people from Hemingway in his day, yet he wrote tight. No Nintendos, no *USA Today*; his competition was his own standard for crisp writing.

No, we write tight because, like virtue, doing so is its own reward. Or, at least, it leads us to good writing, which carries the further rewards of being accepted, paid for, and *read*. Yes, concise writing helps readers fit our words into their schedules and shows respect for the readers and their precious time. But more important, tight writing makes its point — and in its concision and swiftness delivers information and impact.

It is the difference between hitting with a pillow and hitting with a baseball bat. The pillow, soft and fluffy and unshaped. The baseball bat, hard and compact and well defined.

Pillow writing is flabby and boring, and wastes time. It sounds unsure, even evasive. And worst of all, it disrespects the reader — and disrespects the craft of writing itself.

Baseball-bat writing — tight writing — shows confidence, which in turn communicates authority. It is also memorable. (Not to mention quotable.)

Write Tight is about baseball-bat writing, whether you're a poet, a fiction writer, a screenwriter, a nonfiction writer. It is a book about writing with impact and precision. It is *not* a book about sparse, robotic writing. It is *not* about tightwad writing. Rather it is about frugality. Words well spent. You see, tight writing can be flowery, dramatic; it can billow and sashay and go on and on for pages. Tight writing is not by definition short writing. And short writing isn't always tight.

This book is, therefore, not a call for MTV writing, full of quick, flashy cuts from one image to another. It is not a call for *USA Today* writing, summarizing the world in sidebar length. Nor is it a call for writing that panders to "today's short attention span"—because I don't necessarily buy the argument that attention spans have shortened. We may spend less time here, less time there, but is that because of shorter attention spans, or is there another source of the problem? I propose that our tolerance for time-wasters has decreased. If a TV show is wasting our time, turn the channel. If a magazine article is wasting our time, turn the page. And worst of all, if a magazine article is wasting our time, turn on the TV. Wasted words are wasted time. Pertinent, efficient, important words—those are what readers will stick with.

Write Tight uses a broad definition of "lengthy" writing. Flabby writing is any that slows the reader down—anything that *physically* slows the sweep of the eyes across the words, that stands *physically* in the way of the reader's mind absorbing the meaning of the words as quickly as possible.

Traditionally, lengthy writing is defined as verbose writing. Using "redact" instead of "edit," "ecdysiast" instead of "stripper," "at this point in time" instead of "now"—such usage mires the reader in unneeded syllables. "At this point in time": an inch in printed type, a stripe of a phrase; "now": a blip, a whisk of letters. "Lengthy means verbose" is a workable definition, one that concludes that the fewer the words, the better. But it's not the only definition.

You control other writing elements that *physically* impede reading, and understanding. Granted, some of these elements affect the reader's *mental* ability to absorb the material, but however you look at it, you want the reader to spend fifteen physical minutes absorbing your information, laughing at your anecdotes, accepting your point of view, or urging your fictional protagonist to victory—not an hour and a quarter.

So, my definition of lengthy writing also includes verbal brambles that contribute to "mental length," such as:

• Anything that confuses the reader. The convoluted phrase, the big word labeled "dictionary not included," the esoteric and incomplete instructions, the overly clever side remark — anything that forces readers to reread or to pause to figure out what you meant.

• Anything that adds a physical component to understanding what you've written. Extended cross-referencing, asking readers to read something you or someone else wrote in another book or magazine, or otherwise broadening the reading experience beyond the scope of the beginning, middle and end you have set to paper.

• Anything that the reader might naturally resist. A lecture, for instance. No one wants to be preached at, so if your short story fades into a series of didactic pronouncements, the reader, resisting and resenting, will plod through the material. A lecture *feels* long.

• Anything that calls attention to itself. The word that makes the reader pause because it's right, but, well, unusual and distracting; the snappy and clever phrase that giggles in the middle of a funereal article; the sibilant sensual sophisticated saucy alliteration that hisses out of an otherwise workmanlike bit of reportage.

• Anything — words, concepts, whatever — you force readers to slog through even though they don't have to.

Anything, in sum, that impedes the flow of words and sentences. Such problems slow the reading experience. Worse yet, any of them, from verbiage to lectures, can *quicken* the reading experience. Skipping over it is a lot quicker than reading it, yes? Therefore, anything that slows the reader from reaching either your point or the end of the manuscript is ripe for removal.

Ultimately, long or short, terse or flowery, tight writing is unencumbered by dead weight. It carries the reader along, at whatever length, with efficiency, with grace. Consider deadwood words and phrases as the sandbags once used to help control the flight of hot-air balloons. Cast aside the sandbag words and watch the balloon fly. But an odd thing about this balloon we have here. Cast off the sandbags and the balloon carries us only so high. Now, puncture the balloon itself and release the hot air, and we fly even higher.

Dump the dead words in your writing. Release some of its hot air. Watch your ideas fly.

1. The Four Levels of Wordiness and How to Tackle Them

*O*ne of my hobbies is cultivating bonsai, the miniature trees that, full-grown, rarely stand higher than a foot. Bonsai don't provide as much shade as their sixty-foot counterparts, but they are as lovely, and in their grace and compact sweep, even more majestic.

Bonsai are grown carefully and lovingly. They are shaped exactingly and aesthetically. They are pruned regularly and systematically.

So it should be with writing.

Bonsai look and are delicate. But they are not frail. Yes, they require constant tending and shaping and pruning, but the results are hardy, long-living.

So it is with writing.

In this book I will speak of bonsai now and again, not to invoke Eastern mysticism, but to correlate the living art of the bonsai and the living art of a well-shaped, well-pruned manuscript.

With pencil and trowel, then, let's take the bonsai gardener's approaches to attacking wordiness at four levels. We grow graceful bonsai and graceful writing by *selecting what to grow in the first place, trimming the roots, shaping the stem and the branches, and pruning the leaves and shoots.*

Let's examine each level:

Level 1: We grow graceful writing by selecting what to grow in the first place.

The bonsai gardener first chooses the seedling he will groom into his living art. This takes vision: Can the two-inch-high wisteria be trained into a cascade of branches splashing over its planter and reaching swiftly toward the ground? Can the Japanese fir stoop into stoic sweep as if it grew on a rock face, fighting a constant, determined wind?

Your seedlings are the subjects you want to write about. Can your gripe with how the city handles garbage collection be nurtured into a newspaper essay inspiring change in local government? Can a character sketch bloom into novelhood, giving readers insights into interesting new lives? Or are they only gripes, only character sketches?

Carefully select the seedlings of your poetry, fiction, nonfiction, scripts and, yes, advertising and business writing; picture the final product and ask yourself if you should spend time setting it to paper. There is no greater waste of words than in writing about subjects that no one cares about. The 1,000-word article on a subject no one cares about wastes more words than the chatty 3,000-word article that includes 500 words no one cares about.

At least, that's what mathematics would tell us. But the waste is even greater, because that same 1,000-word article wastes more in a philosophical sense than the chatty 60,000-word *book* that could be trimmed by 59,500 words. In terms of pure numbers, one wastes 59,500 words; the other, 1,000 words. In terms of real value—and writing *must* deliver real value, whether informational, inspirational, emotional or otherwise—one wastes most of the time spent reading it; the other, *all* of the time spent reading it. I'd rather wade through 60,000 words with 500 words of value than 1,000 words with no value.

That may be an exaggeration, but it's not idle posturing to self-prove my point. I recently read a book about marketing trends that was 80 to 85 percent self-indulgent, vague, redundant hoo-ha. But in the other 15 percent I found some ideas and some procedures I could put to use in my job at Writer's Digest Books. Granted, I would have preferred that that 15 percent be boiled down to a long 9,000-word article, but I suffered through the bales of chaff to get to the occasional wheat. Better that than trying to nourish myself on whole-chaff bread, no matter how much or how little of it I had to consume.

These are extremes, of course. The goal is to deliver 60,000 words with 60,000 words of value. Or 1,000 words with 1,000 words of value. Whatever the length, you must deliver value.

Valuable writing gives readers as many of the following elements as possible:

• Information. But not just scattered facts—ideally, you will supply information that readers will use, from step-by-step how-to to the latest scientific discoveries to some casual friend-to-friend advice.

• Entertainment. From the so-called pure escapism of popular fiction to laugh-aloud humor to tear-jerking human interest stories.

• Understanding about the world and how it affects them. Analysis, trend projections, what that new federal law *really* means.

Former magazine editor and *Writer's Digest* Nonfiction columnist Art Spikol defines value in a different way, pointing out that writing should address basic human needs: life, health, security (monetary, professional, societal, or related to shelter), prestige/status, sensual stimulation (food, music, physical activity, sports), mental stimulation, relaxation, and altruism. Looked at in this way, you can see how some information can supply value, even if it is only entertainment value (a profile of the star of the latest dance movie, for instance).

Even something so seemingly self-serving as an op-ed piece ("opinion-editorial") must provide value, or it won't be read. Yes, editorial pieces may seek to sway opinion, but they can't do so unless they inform, or at least entertain.

To determine if your writing has value, ask yourself, What will the reader take away from what I'm writing? Offered as example and not as plug: Here at Writer's Digest, both book and magazine divisions, we answer that question when we demand that our books and magazines deliver what we refer to as the three I's and the four T's. Our publications must deliver *Inspiration, Instruction* and *Information*. And they must give readers something they can *Take To The Typewriter*. Always keep in mind what the readers get out of all this. If there's nothing in it for them, they move on.

"What will the reader take away?" is an important question, with an even more important follow-up: "Is what the reader will take away what the reader *wants* to take away?" If readers turn to your fiction for entertainment and you give him page-long treatises on the life cycles of mushrooms, you have failed to deliver value. If, however, those same readers turn to your fiction to immerse themselves in tales that reveal the inner workings of the world (as is often true in mysteries and, by projection, science fiction), details about the fungal world might deliver exactly what they want (though I would suggest that you not clump it all onto a single lecturing page, that you weave it efficiently into the narrative).

A final element of value is freshness. There's no value in old news, anything that might spur readers to react, "We've heard all that before": an essay that only restates previously made points, a historical piece that regurgitates available facts and offers no insights, even clichéd plots and characters in fiction, twist stories where we've all heard the twist before. (Examples: The science fiction story about the lost astronauts on a new planet—their names are Adam and Eve. Or the mystery story in which the detective solves the crime by telling the villain, "I know you hid the dagger under the couch cushions"; the villain responds, "How did you find that out?" With a smirk, the detective says, *"You* just told me.")

To avoid old news, read extensively in your areas of specialization to reduce your chances of repeating what someone else has done.

And avoid repeating yourself. Experiment. Explore new types of writing. Always seek the fresh.

Perceptions of Value

Value can't be measured in absolute terms, because there are two types of value:

- Actual value—which satisfies a need.
- *Perceived* value—which satisfies what the reader *thinks* is a need.

With this in mind, the questions we ask of our writing become, Why will readers care about what I'm telling them? and, Why will they *think* they care? You must have a solid answer for that second question, because perceived value, frankly, is often more important than actual value. Water, for instance, has actual value. It keeps you from dying of thirst. But that doesn't mean you can make the reader drink. Writing with actual value but no perceived value will fail.

The good news is that if it has actual value, you can give it perceived value by clearly demonstrating—with a title, introductory subhead, compelling first paragraph, or other device—exactly why they should *think* they care. It's not my place to tell you exactly how to do that in this book. Leave it at this: The best way to save words is to not spend them when no one is listening.

But don't be embarrassed if your writing addresses only perceived value. Readers are interested, aren't they? They are satisfied by what you've written, aren't they? You've given them what they wanted, haven't you? Every two years or so, *Writer's Digest* runs a story, sometimes the cover story of that particular issue, about copyright and how writers can prevent editors from stealing their writing—

despite the fact that few editors steal writing, and that the chance that any given writer is going to have to call on the long arm of the copyright law is remote. Infringement and theft rarely happen. Yet, readers, especially those early in their careers, think otherwise. So we cover copyright law.

Never lie to your readers, though. Never tell them "what they want to hear." Do, however, talk about what they want you to talk about; once you have their attention, tell them what they need to hear. Readers want to hear about copyright; we talk about copyright. In doing so, we give the facts, and then we tell readers, "You don't have to be all that concerned about copyright, and here's why..."

Danger Areas

Beware projecting your personal ideas of value on your audience. A story—your own or that of someone you know or have met—can be excruciatingly important to you, yet have no impact on or value for the audience you're writing for. I once judged the fiction category of the annual *Writer's Digest* writing competition. I read several stories about the deaths of grandparents, parents and pets. Heartfelt, personal stories that failed at making me the reader care, because they were so personal, so internal. They delivered nothing but the tale of the death itself. They were stories of monumental importance to their authors, of little importance to anyone else. It's easy to fall into the trap of writing such stories; I've fallen into it myself.

My father died shortly before my first book was published. The book was dedicated to him; the dedication thanked him for what he had given me. I had given him no such thanks in person. The dedication was to have made up for years of lost communication between us. But he died, never having read those words. Instead of crying, instead of heading for the therapist's couch, I flushed my emotions into a 2,000-word article. Later, I decided the piece might be appropriate for the Chronicle section of *Writer's Digest*, which I was editing at the time.

Tom Clark was my perceptive managing editor at the time. He read the piece and said, in words more delicate than these: OK, the piece says you're sad. So what? Why should our audience of writers care?

Why indeed? I had written the piece for me. Why should I force my emotions, my frustrations, my guilt, on 120,000 subscribers? Why should I force *me* on them?

I returned to the keyboard and asked myself what this story could possibly deliver to readers. Sadness that I had succeeded as a writer but failed as a son? No.

Strip out the sadness, then. Strip out the personal feelings.

And it was then that the connection hit. I wrote:

My father had depended on his wrenches and his tractors and his super-8 movie cameras to show his love. That's why we waited so long to hug each other. He was too wrapped up in his profession as a mechanic to deal with me as a father.

I had depended on my typewriter and my world of printing presses to show my love. That's why my book was sixteen days and twenty hours too late. I was too. . . .

I could have just told him. I could have just told him. But now I must resort to the typewriter again.

This is my crying.

The words are my crying.

Now I was rising above telling my personal tale of woe. Now I was delivering a lesson useful to most writers, one I had failed to heed: Don't allow your keyboard to do all your communicating for you. Don't allow the keyboard to do your *living* for you.

The too-personal self-examinations crop up so often in fiction that some have become cliché. Nancy McCarthy, former fiction editor of *Woman's World*, wrote an article for *Writer's Digest* called "Never Lead With a Dead Dog" to warn people of the "I-saw-the-dead-dog-on-the-road-this-made-me-think-about-my-own-life" type of story. Then there's the infamous coming of age during college autobiographical novel. They show up in other types of writing, too. For instance, in the early days of word processing, I wrote an article about how the machinery might change not so much how we write but how we approach writing. "The worst danger of all," I noted, "something far more insidious than purely mechanical idiosyncrasies and matters of keyboard paranoia, is a problem I've noticed in literally hundreds of submissions to *Writer's Digest* from writers who have just purchased word-processing systems. Let's call it the Freelance Writer's Law of Instant Technology, Write-About-What-You-Know Corollary: THE FIRST THING WRITERS WANT TO DO AFTER GETTING IN- VOLVED WITH PERSONAL COMPUTERS IS WRITE AN ARTICLE

ABOUT GETTING INVOLVED WITH PERSONAL COMPUTERS."
So, as long as we're asking questions, let's ask one more: Are you
talking about yourself, or are you teaching the reader something
(other than about yourself)?

Remember, though, that you measure value against the writing's
intended audience. If the writing has value only to you, but you are
the intended audience, you have succeeded. If you wrote that intimate
essay about your family difficulties, and it makes you feel better —
you have succeeded as a writer. If you wrote that love poem for an
audience of one, that memoir for your close family members only,
that "in-joke" humor piece for your poker buddies, and they respond,
you have succeeded as a writer. Period, exclamation point. Good writing
serves its audience. It needn't be published to be good; it needn't
even be read by anyone else to be good.

Level 2: We grow graceful writing by trimming its roots.

The bonsai gardener knows that the larger the root system of a
plant, the larger the plant grows. A smaller root system limits the
nutrients available to the plant, and stunts the tree's growth. (If we
could only teach the trees to smoke cigarettes, all this would be so
much simpler. . . .) The bonsai's roots are limited by the size of its
planter, and the gardener removes the tree from its soil every two
years or so to cut away additional root growth.

The roots of your writing lie in the range of what that writing
covers. Trim the roots, narrow the range of coverage, and limit the
manuscript's "nutrients" — the ideas, concepts and source material
that feed into it. Do so, and you limit the size of the resulting
manuscript itself.

This isn't a matter of starving either bonsai or reader, of holding
out on the reader, or of doing limited research so you'll have less to
deliver. It's a matter of defining very clearly from the beginning
exactly what you want the manuscript to accomplish. It's a matter of
focus. What are you going to focus on?

Many writers err by trying to cover too much territory. They
query a baseball magazine and say, "I'd like to write about changes
in baseball over the years." They propose a novel to a publisher and
say, "I'd like to write a novel about evangelism." Those are some
huge roots. You can write forever on those topics. Snip away at

them. Focus them—by asking, What about . . . ? <u>Ask it again and again.</u>

What about changes in baseball over the years? How about the fact that strike zones are different these days? *What about the strike zones being different?* How about "Umpires Are Demolishing the Legal Strike Zone," an article that appeared in *Baseball Digest?*

What about evangelism? How about how it can be misused? *What about how it can be misused?* How about the people who misuse it? *What about the people who misuse evangelism?* How about *Elmer Gantry?*

Two wildly different examples, but you see how focused ideas have led to focused manuscripts. Focus is also known in the world of freelance writing as angle or slant. In other worlds, such as the world of business writing, it's known more simply as your point, what you're trying to say.

<u>Identify exactly what you're trying to say. Then, identify who you're trying to say it to.</u> The combination of these elements (which feeds back to the whole matter of value in a manuscript) dictates your focus.

For example, I have written several articles about another of my hobbies: pinball. Pinball is a pretty big root system. So, *What about pinball?* For the *Cincinnati Enquirer* Sunday magazine and its southwestern Ohio readers, the fact that the first patented pinball machine was created by a Cincinnati resident around the time of the Civil War. For *Collectibles Illustrated* and its audience interested in the nostalgic side of collecting, the growth of the pinball-collecting hobby. For *Questar* and its science fiction-oriented readers, the science fiction themes depicted on pinball machines. And so on.

Define the manuscript's focus before you begin writing it (and definitely before you query any editors about it). Decide what should and should *not* be covered.

Decide, too, the range of coverage within your focus. Take "Umpires Are Demolishing the Legal Strike Zone." The article itself, over two brief pages, theorizes that some baseball greats would have had lackluster careers if they were playing today: Many of pitcher Jim Palmer's strikes would be called balls today; notorious high-ball hitter Ted Williams would have struck out more and hit fewer home runs had today's low strike zone been in force during his day. Had the writer then brought in the point that many fans are upset with the strike zone, he would have had to convince us of that point. He couldn't just say it. He'd have to cite fan polls or quote some season ticket holders, and in doing so he'd have to convince us that the polls were valid, and that the quoted fans had enough knowledge of the sport for the reader to give them credence.

So, by introducing the fans into the article—which certainly would have been appropriate, and within the bounds of the article's focus— the article gets longer. For every new idea, concept or topic you inject into your manuscript, you must devote additional space to its introduction and explication. If you introduce a new character into a short story, you must describe her, tell who she is and how she relates to the character and the plot. That takes words. If you quote another source in your nonfiction article, you must explain who he is, what makes him credible, and how what he says relates to everything else you're discussing.

Level 3: We grow graceful writing by shaping its stem and branches.

The most commonly known method of shaping bonsai is to twist wire around the young branches, and then bend both wire and branches into the intended shape. But a subtler and often preferred method is to snip away superfluous branches and reveal the whole plant's inner shape in what remains.

This is the same principle, I suppose, espoused by Michelangelo, if memory serves: Sculpting, he contended, was a matter of revealing the statue within the marble block by chipping away everything that wasn't the statue. Or the same principle that Elmore Leonard referred to when he said, "I try to leave out the parts that people skip."

As you grow the writing, as you put the words to paper, you bring shape and direction to the manuscript. There is but one direction—toward the range of coverage you determined when trimming the roots. This shape and direction are the angle and focus of the manuscript; anything that doesn't contribute to the inner shape—the angle and focus—is superfluous.

To reveal your writing's inner shape, use the following exercise: In a couple of sentences, define the *goal* of your writing. Categorize it. Answer these questions: What drives your writing? What is its central purpose? What do readers expect from it? What, once more, is its real and/or its perceived value?

Next, list two secondary goals. What gives the piece added value?

What gives it texture? What makes it interesting? fun to read? something the reader will enjoy as well as benefit from?

For example, I define the goals of this book this way.

Primary goal: to teach techniques of writing with as few words as possible.

Secondary goals: 1) to give insight into the language, and how the very structure of the language can be employed to keep writing trim and efficient, and 2) to keep these matters of language use, which are often picayune, from becoming boring, so that the subject remains as lively as the language itself.

Do you have additional secondary goals for your manuscript? List them, too—but consider them carefully. Are you trying to accomplish too much? Will a manuscript with so many goals become muddled? Will your writing become more effective if you are less ambitious?

With the goals down on paper, examine your secondary goals. Do they support the primary goals?

A simplistic way of looking at this exercise is to say that the primary goal defines your content; the secondary goals define your form, how you present the content. You must synchronize the primary and the secondary. Form must complement style and vice versa.

Say you're writing a mystery, and your primary purpose is: Identify, through detection, the murderer of a community leader. Your secondary purpose should not be to "Use my sense of humor to get the reader laughing out loud." It *can* be to "Weave humor into the storytelling to make the detective more sympathetic and the story more interesting." Big laughs might result—but humor, or any other secondary purpose, can't be an isolated goal.

I say that viewing primary/secondary goals in the light of form/ content is simplistic because the form/content model doesn't cover other possibilities. You might think that form should not be a primary purpose, but consider that some forms dictate your central purpose: A mystery must have something along the lines of what I've just described as its primary goal; an annual report must have informing shareholders of the financial standing of the company as its primary goal. The secondary purposes then begin to define how this mystery, this annual report, whatever, will differ from the others. A secondary purpose of an annual report might be to pump up shareholder confidence in a company being hit hard by recession, or it might be to generate support for planned expansion of the company.

And form can itself be a central purpose: for instance, when you write haiku or a sonnet. Content becomes a secondary purpose, a *subordinate* purpose, because as I hinted above, form can dictate content. The haiku dictates pastoral subjects; the sonnet fairly demands examination of love; the annual report, numbers; humor, crispness. In an episode of the animated cartoon hit *The Simpsons*, child prodigy Lisa Simpson enters a patriotic essay contest sponsored by a magazine thinly disguised as *Reading Digest*. When Lisa arrives at the contest finals, we briefly (of course) spot a banner proclaiming, "Brevity is . . . wit." I think even Shakespeare would have giggled. "Brevity is the soul of wit," quoth he. "Even more brevity is the soul of parody," quoth the Simpsons. (On the other hand—and in things linguistic there's almost always an other hand—much of Dave Barry's humor hinges on his "failures" at brevity.)

Consider, then, the dictates of your goals, not only what they demand you include, but also what they demand you *exclude*.

Now that you're satisfied with what you're trying to accomplish, judge what you write, sentence by sentence, paragraph by paragraph, against its goals. Let's go back to our example story, about the umpires demolishing the legal strike zone. The article talks about how the modern strike zone is lower than it was in the 1950s. The goals of the article are to prove that the zone has indeed moved and demonstrate how that has changed the game. You do that with information and numbers and quoted opinion from people involved with the game, primarily umpires, batters, catchers, pitchers and the occasional manager. You don't do that with opinions about how the height of outfield fences has changed over the years, a history of the introduction of artificial turf, or a funny Yogi Berra quote about how umpires dress.

Now, in a single word, define what you're delivering within the form you have chosen. Does your manuscript deliver, for example:

- Information
- Atmosphere, mood
- Entertainment

Circle everything in the manuscript that serves that goal. If you end up with a couple of circles per page, perhaps you are giving your primary goal short shrift. Worse yet, perhaps you're crowding out your core material with other stuff.

Also read the manuscript with a less precise eye: Ask questions of your manuscript and your goals. Are you, for example, seeking to deliver information? What you deliver should therefore not only inform, but it should also *feel* like information. Everything that doesn't *feel* like it's giving information, or supporting the information that you're not giving, should be excluded. Jokes and asides, for instance, likely won't inform; nor will they have the crisp, direct feel of information.

Or are you seeking to entertain? Strip away all unessential material that doesn't entertain.

A quicker bit of advice: Just strip away all that's unessential.

Level 4: We grow graceful writing by pruning its leaves and shoots.

About once a year, during the growing season, the bonsai gardener snips away new growth—sprouting leaves and young branches. Such minor tending has major benefit to the plant: It retains the plant's shape and proper size, and it directs the nutrients flowing through the plant toward the new growth area back into the stem and the main branches, strengthening them and increasing their bulk.

Let's consider individual words, stray sentences and unneeded digressions as the leaves and the branches of our carefully tended manuscript. Clearing out the unnecessary growth not only gives our manuscript the trim shape we want, but also directs the strength and energy of the manuscript into its core. It also directs the readers' attention (which, I might argue, is the ultimate strength and energy of any manuscript) to the core of the manuscript, undistracted as the readers are by verbiage, no matter how lovely it may be.

Now, in chapter two and beyond, let's look more closely at the leaves and branches we'll be trimming.

2. Sixteen Types of Wordiness and How to Trim Them

I'm lousy at yardwork. I can't tell the weeds from the flowers around the house, so I let them all grow. If I could identify the weeds, tending my yard would be a lot easier.

So it is with weed words, the stuff that grows so hardily in your manuscripts. Trouble is, like some weeds, these parasitic undergrowths can deceive you. They're pretty, and they don't look like weeds.

Wordweeds, prunable leaves and branches—whatever organic analogy you subscribe to—fall into these general categories:

1. The redundant
2. The already understood
3. The empty
4. The evasive (intentional or otherwise)
5. The passive
6. The weak, the noncommittal and the hesitant
7. The affected
8. The circuitous
9. The self-indulgent
10. The overkill
11. The inflated and the deflated
12. The invisible and therefore unnecessary
13. The imprecise
14. The clever and the show-offy
15. The nonsensical
16. The beautiful

Each of these types can affect your manuscript at each of the four levels of growing graceful writing described in chapter one:

Selecting what to grow in the first place (idea selection), trimming the roots (manuscript planning and focusing the range of coverage), shaping the stem and the branches (writing to feed into the manuscript's focus), and pruning the leaves and branches (trimming and revising). Take the redundant, for instance. It can show up at these levels, in these forms (as well as others):

• Idea selection. "Old news," such as that described in chapter one, is sweepingly redundant. "So tell me something new," readers subconsciously grouse, if they're reading at all.

• Manuscript planning. There's little sense in repeating, for instance, your source material. Suppose in writing an article about changes in rural America, you plan to profile four small towns. Will you (and your sources) be repeating yourself after the third town? Will the repetition set in after the first?—perhaps *one* can represent all the rest.

• Writing to the manuscript's focus. Unless you watch carefully, you can spend three anecdotes to support a single point. The tales aren't themselves redundant, but a point made three times is.

• Trimming and revising. Pesky tautologies simply clutter things up saying "mental telepathy" when "telepathy" is enough or saying "past achievement" when "achievement" itself communicates that it happened in the past.

In listing types of wordiness, I'm not trying to establish a classification of mutually exclusive phyla and species. Think of the list instead as a family tree of flab. In families, you have siblings, and you have third cousins twice removed. Some family members are simply more closely related to each other than are others. So it is with wordiness. On this family tree appears what I've termed "the politically correct," for instance. It's a separate member of the family all to itself, but it's a child of "the affected," a sibling of "the faddish," and a third cousin twice removed of "the evasive." So if I've classified your favorite flabby writing as "the redundant" and you believe that it's really better labeled as "the already understood," just think of it as visiting grandma's for the holidays, and it'll go home to its proper list as soon as it finishes the apple pie.

Let's spend some time, then, with each member of the family. The sixteen types of flab in writing are:

1. The Redundant

No sense in being repetitious, and otherwise repeating yourself.

Redundancy is so prevalent a problem in speech that we have several words to describe it: "Redundancy" itself is superfluous repetition; a "tautology" is, well, superfluous repetition; "pleonasm" is using more words than necessary to get your ideas across; "prolixity" is using more words than necessary to get your ideas across; "circumlocution" is using more words than necessary to get your ideas across . . .

Are we seeing a pattern here? How appropriate that we use redundant words to describe redundancy. Of course, I'm oversimplifying, because the words are not synonymous. "Circumlocution" denotes using a lot of words as a means of evasion, "prolixity" means injecting material that has nothing to do with the subject at hand, and "pleonasm" is using words that in and of themselves add nothing to the sentence (such as the phrase "in and of themselves" in *this* sentence).

Then there's "verbosity," a good umbrella term for wordiness in general, and such a nice way of saying "being a windbag."

So, to avoid further being a windbag myself, here are ways to avoid redundancy:

Big, and Important

On the large scale, cover a topic once, then move on. If you're profiling a local businessperson, for example, discuss the history of her success once at the appropriate place in the manuscript. Let's say you cover history as background in the first couple of pages, then return to it near the middle of the manuscript, then allow a little more of the rise to power to slip in near the end. I would wager that you're repeating something—if it's not significant information, then it's certainly setup information—the information needed to three times establish separate sections of the manuscript as history.

Go through your manuscript, asking yourself, What's the point of this sentence/paragraph/chapter? If you find that more than one of those units seeks to accomplish the same thing, perhaps you can combine them. Perhaps one or more can be cut altogether.

Reducing multiple coverage of information, concepts or topics gives you two benefits. The obvious is concision and attendant clarity. The other, credibility and authority. Repetition, especially in the form of backtracking and revisiting points, signals disorganization at best.

At worst, it signals that you're floundering, that you don't know where you're going next.

Chapters three and four outline ways to identify multiple coverage.

Little, But Also Important

On the small scale, avoid the small-scale redundancy, the tautology. Tautologies pair synonymous words. "But" and "however" mean the same thing, so the phrase "but however" is redundant. A moment is by its nature brief, so we needn't speak of a brief moment to be understood. You don't have to tell me the reason why when you can tell me the reason, or when you can tell me why.

Tautologies, sometimes called "baby puppies," come in these forms:

* The tautological adjective: a small smidgeon, annual birthday, glowing ember
* The tautological double adjective: the pure unadulterated truth, a teeny tiny portion, the itsy bitsy spider
* The tautological adverb: protrude out, rise up, dash quickly
* The tautological double noun: Sahara Desert, cash money, switchblade knife
* The tautological double conjunction: and also, but however
* The tautological pair: each and every, forever and ever, the one and only

To keep these puppies from nipping at your ankles:

1. Familiarize yourself with the enemy—and there are thousands of them. To list tautologies at length here would mire us in a long digression. For an alphabetical listing of common redundancies, see the Baedeker of the Redundant on page 185.

2. Read your copy carefully. Pause at the "invisible" words. "And" is invisible; "also" is invisible; "and also" is neither more nor less visible, unless you're looking for it. Pause at two-word combinations. If you encounter a double noun, drop one to see if the sentence still makes sense; if an adverb-verb or adjective-noun, drop the modifier to see if you lose anything. If you can drop "advance" from "advance planning," do it.

3. Maintain an active vocabulary that is not only broad but also deep. Learn not just what words mean, but what they imply, what they embrace. Read not only for the sake of the writing but also for the sake of the words; read to learn words. And don't rely purely on your ear and on the context of speech and of writing to educate you about word meanings. Look words up, but don't stop there. Hunt words. As you read dictionary definitions, dig into their origins, their evolution, and their present scope.

You perhaps never looked up "pedal." Common word, originating from the Latin root "ped," or foot. So why do we say "foot pedal"? (As opposed to the elbow pedal?) Why do we note a "pedestrian on foot"?

Another example: You know what "starve" means. Starvation means extreme hunger, right? But until you look it up, do you realize that "to starve" means "to die of hunger"? *That* is extreme hunger. Therefore, saying "starve to death" is redundant. The concept of death is embraced by the word "starve."

Redundancy occurs when extra words either directly repeat what another word means or *implies*. A couple of examples of each type of etymological toe-stepping:

• Direct repetition of meaning: Facts are true, so the phrase "true facts" works under "false pretenses," a phrase wrought from the same verbose construction. "I" and "myself" are the same person, so "I myself" doesn't make me any more me than I already am.

• Repetition of implication: By strict definition, facts don't have to be known to be facts. There are plenty of facts about the universe—the number of stars, how the universe began, how much wood could a woodchuck chuck if a woodchuck could chuck wood. Still, "facts" implies information that we know, so in most cases, "known facts" and "established facts" are redundant.

That in mind, let your love of words allow you to pay attention to the various concepts and meanings that words imply or define:

Words can imply or define time. Including:

• The past. "We did that before in the past." In that sentence, "in the past" could go, as "before" signals that it happened in the past. More important, the past tense signals that it happened in the past, so "before" can go, as well. "We did that."

• The future. Foreseeing the future is so much more possible than foreseeing the past. And advance planning is more efficient than planning after the fact. And there's no sense in noting that you will get your car repaired in the future; "will" slips the sentence into the future tense.

• The present. You've heard one redundancy dozens of times: Now playing at a theatre near you! As opposed to "Yesterday playing at a theatre near you!" or "Tomorrow playing at a theatre near you!" The present tense implies "now." "You are reading this" is as clear as "You are reading this now"—unless the "now" serves a function. For example, "You are reading this now, though you were reading the newspaper a few minutes ago." ("Now" helps signal a change, but "though" signals contrast, so even in that case you could argue that "now" is unnecessary.)

Words can imply or define continuance. In "The situation still remains the same," the word "remains" implies what "still" needn't restate. And just as the present tense signals "now," it can also signal the continuing nature of a situation. So "remains" is giving you two signals—verb tense and meaning.

Words can imply or define permanence, or lack thereof. There's no such thing as a temporary reprieve; if it's not temporary, it's permanent, and therefore it's a pardon.

Words can imply or define inclusion or exclusion. A "pride" is a group of lions, so "pride of lions" is redundant. "Pride" *in*cludes lions and *ex*cludes, say, chickens. And a lot of other things. "Pie and ice cream a la mode" piles ice cream upon ice cream—"pie a la mode" includes the ice cream.

Words can imply or define beginnings or endings, firsts or lasts. "Began" implies being the first in "first began"; "created" implies being the first in "first created." Or, at the other end of things, we come to the "end result." So much better than the beginning result. (I'll concede the possibility of "middle results," though.) So, too, with "end product."

Words can imply or define potentiality—or impossibility. A candidate can't be a "potential candidate" unless he or she is not yet a candidate, but *might* be (a candidate for a candidate?). So, too, "possible candidate." How could you possibly disagree? Well, you *could*, but since "could" signals possibility, saying "could possibly" is redundant.

Words can imply or define destination, direction or origin. To make forward progress in concision, eliminate "forward" in this sentence (unless you believe going backward can be considered a type of progress). So it is with advancing forward and retreating back. Or returning back, regressing back, and so on.

Words can imply or define results. If you pass a test, you automatically "passed the test successfully." If you weave something, your materials will be together when you're done, so "weave together" is wordy.

Words can imply or define the "how" of themselves. That is, they express so specifically an action or a thing that *how* the action is taken or *how* the thing exists needn't be stated. They obviate many of the adverbs or adjectives you might use with them. A couple of phrases I encountered in books recently: "Jot down quickly one or two words . . ." I would venture that most jotting is done fairly quickly, especially if only a couple of words are being jotted. "Jot" doesn't specifically imply "quickly," but readers won't expect laborious jotting, so "quickly" adds little to the sentence. Another example: "He slipped carefully from the shadows." If you're skulking in the shadows, it's doubtful that you're doing it without some measure of care. Careless slipping happens on wet floors and banana peels; again, the adverb adds nothing to reader understanding. Or consider the phrase "forcible revolution." If one revolts, one rarely does it passively; the very nature of revolution implies that it was likely achieved how? Forcibly.

Words can imply or define their own nature. No need to say "amounts of money" because money is measured in amounts. No need to say "few in number" because few describes things that can be numbered. In the sentence, "The time was 10:30," 10:30 by convention and definition is a time, so we needn't call it that. The same applies to such sentences as "The city was New York" and "The problem was a flat tire."

Here, a quote from a newspaper story about the movie *Hook*: "Spielberg's preoccupation with Peter Pan dates back several years to a time when he . . ." As opposed to "a *place* when he . . ."? "When" implies time; you understand time because of "when," so delete "a time." You can likely do similar trimming of other phrasings in which the subordinating conjunction implies what it describes:

• *a person* who: "John Wilkes Booth was the person who shot President Lincoln." Better: "John Wilkes Booth was who shot President Lincoln."

• *a place* where: "The Ford Theater is the place where President Lincoln was shot." Better: "Dallas is where President Kennedy was shot."

Now, look at the two "Better" examples above, and, by taking the concept of implication and relationship a step further, we can make them even better. "John Wilkes Booth was who . . ." Well, Booth was a person. A person is a who (as opposed to a what or a why). That Booth was a who is understood, and we can eliminate it. "John Wilkes Booth shot President Lincoln." Similarly, the Ford Theater is a where; thus, with a little rearranging to eliminate "where," we end up with "President Lincoln was shot in the Ford Theater."

Watch for similar constructions that use reflexive nouns: "Secretariat was a horse that won the Triple Crown." Secretariat and "a horse" are the same thing.

Sometimes the two types of reflexives can land in the same sentence, ballooning it nearly endlessly. "Tom is an example of a man who mows his lawn twice a week." This can be trimmed considerably to "Tom mows his lawn twice a week."

Words can imply or define the absolute. Many words describing ultimates or absolutes imply or define either/or situations. Either you're pregnant, or you're not. There are no dimmer switches for such words, no sliding scales. Either something is demolished or it's not. Totally demolished is redundant; partially demolished is nonsensical. Yet, writers continue to try to make absolutes more absolute. (Nothing can be more absolute.) For instance: "jam-packed full" (full is full); "totally abolished" (you can't partially abolish); "absolutely necessary" (it's necessary or it's not).

Or they try to make absolutes less absolute. (That's another impossibility: If it's less than absolute, it's simply not absolute.) For instance: "a little unique" (turn it into a synonym—"a little one-of-a-kind"), or "somewhat possible" (possible by any degree is still possible). These are the hoary examples. Look for other instances where the same reasoning applies. For example: "That notion is a bit laughable." Either something is laughable or it isn't. Maybe you can laugh at it a bit—there are degrees of laughter—but if you can laugh at something, even a quick little snicker, it's laughable.

Now, there are ways of indicating degrees of such words. Something might be *almost* unique, *almost* starved, *almost* a vacuum, *almost* laughable, but they can't be somewhat unique, partially starved, kind of sort of a vacuum, or mostly laughable.

Also, some words are not absolutes, yet the reader will assume the absolute unless you say otherwise. "I liquidated my assets" says everything that wordier versions do—such as "I liquidated *all* my assets" or "I *totally* liquidated my assets." What's more, sometimes other signals point to entirety. In the sentence "The book devotes an entire chapter to selecting a muffler," the word "entire" is unneeded. The reader will assume correctly, by the word "devotes," that all of the chapter covers mufflers.

A related matter: If your choice is "all" or nothing, often nothing is better. In a sentence like "I'm glad you're all here," the word "all" adds nothing. Usually, when you refer to something, or do something, readers will assume you mean all unless you tell them otherwise. For example: "I ate all my dinner." Better is "I ate my dinner."

Similarly, other expressions of entirety are often superfluous— "His whole speech bothered me," "I vetoed the entire proposal"— unless you mean to stress the entirety: "He ate the whole pie!" The glutton.

Finally, words imply or define many other things too numerous to list here. Suffice it to say that you should let words do their own work. Words have managed to survive and to communicate without your help for some time now; they don't need your intrusion now.

2. The Already Understood

The redundant describes unnecessary repetition of items on a page. But repetition can take place on a less concrete level, such as that between writing and reader—when what's on the page repeats what's in the reader's head. This is closely related to some commonsense advice about writing tight: Don't state the obvious. But here we're digging deeper. We are allowing ourselves concision by employing what readers understand about the language and the work it does, about the physical world, about themselves, about what things are and what they are not, and about what you the writer are trying to accomplish.

Let's examine each of those areas more closely.

Don't repeat what readers understand about the language and the work it does. Language and its construction implies relationships and imparts meanings that you don't have to reiterate. Three quick examples:

• When I write "Do your homework," the sentence's object, "You," is understood. I don't have to write "You do your homework" to be understood.

• "Then" in "if/then" constructions is understood and is usually deletable. "If you start a sentence or phrase with 'if,' *then* you can often delete 'then.'"

• "That" is often understood, when it serves (grammatically speaking) as a subordinator. "You said that you went to the store" and "You said you went to the store" are interchangeable.

In fact, English could borrow a little concision from Spanish, a language that makes some relationships within a sentence obvious— and then allows you to speak more quickly. To say "I am a writer" in Spanish, you say, "Soy escribre"—literally, "Am writer." You don't have to say "Yo soy uno escribre," which is "I am a writer" translated literally. The verb conjugation for "to be" is "soy" for the first person—it applies to no other case, just as "am" in English applies to no other case. I would never say "He am a writer" or "You am a writer." So why can't we say in English "Am a writer"?—the "am" signals that *I* am saying it. The Spanish do. They also eliminate the indefinite article. I can't be two writers, so why use the "a"? (And

I'll leave the discussion at that, because am spending too much time on it.)

Much of what's understood about the language relates to the word definitions and implications discussed under "The Redundant." For example, verb tense often tells you what you need to know about the when of the sentence, so you can eliminate other indicators of when, either the obvious ones such as "now" and "before" or the less obvious ones such as "still." Verb tense and context imply the when; readers infer the when, readers *understand* the when.

In these cases, grammar and etymology imply what can go unstated. On a larger level, situation and context imply what can go unstated. For instance, while hooking up my son's Nintendo (yes, I bought him books that Christmas, too), I disconnected the cable input from the TV, making the screen as fuzzy as my son seems to be when he plays Nintendo. "Did you pull the wrong wire, Dad?" he said with typical six-and-a-half-year-old confidence in my grasp of electronics. "You're not supposed to do that."

I peered at him from the wire web parlor that the electronic spider had invited me into and said, "Can you think of a time when you *are* supposed to pull the wrong wire?" I may not be able to beat him at Super Mario World, but I have a slight edge in that language-use game for the moment.

The situation, the phrase "wrong wire," and the intent behind my son's question ("How the heck did you foul that up, Dad?") make it obvious that you're not supposed to pull the wrong wire.

A writing example is a phrase you see in various forms almost daily in newspapers: "A new study released Friday. . ." If they were releasing *old* studies, it would be worth noting. We can assume that a study being released is new—delete "new." This redundancy happens frequently. A new shopping center will be built next summer. As opposed to an old shopping center? Again, though, remember that "new" can have a function in such cases. If the shopping center being built replaces an existing shopping center, saying "A new shopping center will be built" signals that it is a *replacement*. But there's no excuse for something like "New construction on the road begins next week," whether the road exists and is being repaired.

Another example, as the TV movie-of-the-week people would tell us, "ripped from today's headlines": "Will Clark and Robby Thompson both homered." What does "both" tell us that "Will Clark and Robby Thompson homered" does not? It doesn't tell us that these baseball stars accomplished their feat at different times—that's obvious in this context, because no duo has ever hit a single home run working together.

And a third: "President Bush is on the campaign trail with an eye on getting reelected." The phrase "with an eye on getting reelected" can be deleted—again, for "obvious reasons."

Don't repeat what readers understand about the physical world. In a John Caldwell cartoon labeled "Beginning Food Critic," a writer sits at a restaurant table, his right hand wrist-deep in a bowl while with his left he jots onto a notepad: "The bisque, though a bit hot, was sufficiently deep and wet."

The humor in this cartoon keys off a couple of concision-related problems, including stating the obvious (doing so wastes space, and condescends to readers) and not directly addressing what the audience needs and wants to know (no reader is going to finish a review wondering how deep the soup was). But important here is that some things about the physical world can go unsaid because of what the reader understands about that world. Readers know that soup is wet, or it isn't soup yet.

That's a matter of description. We don't have to describe lakes as having water or rocks as being hard or the sky as being blue. We know holes and space and vacuums are empty. Readers know that those things have those qualities.

But there's also the matter of implication. What does the physical world imply? Rocks imply hardness. It works in the opposite direction. Hardness can imply rocks. And you can use that relationship to communicate description without spelling everything out.

For details on how to employ such relationships of implication, see "Putting It All Together: Writing Light" on page 155.

Don't repeat what readers understand about themselves. Sometimes I believe colloquialism underlies my interest in brevity. Back in my home state Wisconsin, I can ask questions like "Do you want to come with?", and my meaning is perfectly clear.

Ninety-eight percent of you now reading this would express the same thought by saying, "Do you want to come with *me*?" But in my stomping grounds, the *me* is colloquially unstated. Why should I state "me"?—after all, it is me who is asking. There's no possibility of confusion. I couldn't be asking "Do you want to come with (Fred)?" (In part because I would then say, "Do you want to *go* with?")

And when I use the command form to say, "Come with," both *you* and *me* are understood. The point is that, when I address other Wisconsinites, I can speak our lingo.

Do the same in your writing; shape your word choice to suit your audience and you can take advantage of opportunities to streamline your sentences. (The bonus is that by doing so you also build credibility and rapport with readers.)

This means you can use:

• Abbreviations and acronyms. Write to a medical audience, and you can snap off references to PTO. That's "planned time off"— "vacation" to you and me. Sometimes arcane abbreviations and acronyms become a part of the language. We have "Zone Improvement Plan codes," or, more commonly, "zip codes." We almost daily refer to what was once a deep scientific term, "Light Amplification by Stimulated Emission of Radiation," or the now-common "laser," in relation to everything from eye surgery to CD players.

• Shortened forms. A "code" in a hospital is short for "code blue," the emergency alert phrase for a life-threatening situation.

• Colloquialisms. Writing in, for instance, *Milwaukee Magazine*, I could refer to a "bubbler," while most anywhere else I'd have to write of a "water fountain."

• Jargon. If I were writing to an audience of police officers, I might speak of an attempt to surveil a suspect, a delightful back formation (a linguistic term for removing an affix from a word to create a new word) I picked up while serving on a grand jury. "To surveil" is much shorter than saying "to conduct a surveillance," though I might argue that the stretched-out locution of conducting a surveillance is more tedious and more passive than surveilling, and thus is truer to the action being described.

But use such argot, as I warned before, *as appropriate*. Don't become insulated; these code words exclude far more readers than they include.

And don't get tangled in your own telegraphy. Abbreviations, for instance, offer a special trap—the hidden redundancy. For example, if you're addressing an audience that knows that NHL stands for National Hockey League, you can also assume that they will be amused if you refer to "an NHL hockey game" — there are, after all, not many NHL football games. "Hockey" has been repeated in that phrase, one time deceptively so.

More important than using the vocabulary of the audience is using its *language*. Speak more than the lingo. Speak the cadence, the rhythm, the timbre of the audience. Adjust the formality, level of locution and expansiveness of your prose to what they expect. It's kind of like how my own speech changes when I visit my mother. You wouldn't hear an "ain't" or a "got no" out of my mouth except when I'm at home, where the local grammar requirements aren't nearly as stringent as they are, say, at an editorial meeting in a publishing house. If I speak formally to my mater, she begins to wonder what the hell is wrong with me instead of listening to me (she would, for instance, ask what the heck "mater" meant — as would a lot of people, now that I think about it).

Find out how your audience thinks. Read the magazines they read (presumably including the one you intend to write for). Speak directly to them. Discover not only the words they use, but also how they use those words. Let your words resonate with theirs.

These verbal resonances may or may not reduce the physical length of your prose. Informality, for instance, can contract prose (saying "The cuts will impact you" is more informal than "The cuts will have an impact on you") or expand it (colloquialisms tend to balloon language — such as saying "a whole lot more" instead of "much more"). But whether bequeathing length or concision to the prose, verbal resonances reduce mental length.

Don't repeat what readers understand about what things are — and what they are not. Avoid identifying nouns — people, places, things — that need no identification. Sometimes such identification is blatant, tagging the noun with a descriptive phrase. For instance: "The Empire State Building, a tall building in New York, is . . ." Or "Florence Nightingale, the legendary nurse . . ." — as opposed to Florence Nightingale, the mechanic who fixes your carburetor? Sometimes the identification slips in before the noun. For instance: "Vivian Leigh starred in the movie *Gone With the Wind*." There's no need to mention that it's a movie, since there's not much chance Leigh starred in *Gone With the Wind* the book, the Cliff's Notes or the board game.

Redundant identifiers are related to other redundancies, such as the reflexive descriptors I discussed earlier in this chapter. We might rephrase the above example about Vivian Leigh's movie credits as *"Gone With the Wind* is a movie starring Vivian Leigh" to see the reflexive pattern we can edit out.

Don't repeat what readers understand about what you the writer are trying to accomplish. I believe that you should rely on what the reader understands, and not spell out everything.

Now, let's strip that sentence down. First, scrap the introduction: *I believe that.* If I didn't believe it, why would I be giving you the advice? Yes, there might be reasons for saying, "I believe that." If it's to clarify that the viewpoint is "I" instead of someone else. If it's important to clarify that I'm expressing belief rather than fact (though it's generally understood that advice is based on belief rather than fact). This leaves us with: *You should rely on what the reader understands, and not spell out everything.*

Next, let's scrap "you should." Doing so converts what remains to command form: *Rely on what the reader understands....* Command form implies *you,* and if you trust me as the writer you'll know that I wouldn't ask you to do something that you *shouldn't* do.

Yet, such constructions do have their purposes. I can argue that you could delete "remember to" or "don't forget to" in commands and instructions because there's little chance you'd tell readers something you want them to forget. But such phrasings soften commands. "Don't forget to do the dishes" is friendlier and less intimidating than "Do the dishes." "I think you should seek professional help" is less strident and more personal than "Seek professional help." Just make sure you're not being soft when you don't need to.

Making Yourself Understood

But hesitate before deleting something because "it's understood." Take care to trim what the audience understands, not what you understand. If there's a chance your audience does not know that the Empire State is a tall building in New York, don't slap yourself on the forehead and say, "How can they be so ignorant?" If removing the phrase "I believe" from a sentence risks muddying or disguising the source of the opinion, leave it in. Tell readers all they need to know.

3. The Empty

Empty words, phrases and sentences are the excelsior of language, the fluff you stuff into boxes to cushion their important contents. And like excelsior, empty locutions are fun to discard.

Trashing the Empty

Technically, empty words are symptoms of pleonasms, and they include:

Empty modifiers that sap power from your words. Primarily I mean "very" and its variations, including "extremely," "really," "generally," "usually," "basically," "awfully," "actually," "literally," "kind of," "rather," "pretty much," "quite," "a bit," "certainly," "essentially," "ultimately," "inevitably," "more or less," "for the most part," "mainly," "mostly," "as a rule," "somewhat," "by large measure."

These modifiers can harm manuscripts in a number of ways:

• They can add pure deadwood. What does saying "I'm *very* outraged about this!" do that saying "I'm outraged about this!" does not?

• They can be the same as a basketball coach buying elevator shoes for a jockey when a basketball player should have been hired in the first place. "It was awfully cold" is a jury-rigged way of saying, "It was frigid."

• They can make the reader laugh. "The dog was *extremely* dead."

• They can signal evasion. "The idea is *a bit* ridiculous."

• They can signal condescension. "The idea is *rather* ridiculous." OK, let's make fun of the idea *and* sound smarmy while we're at it.

• They can confuse the reader. "We've radically redesigned the package *somewhat*."

Empty introductions. How many times have you heard chatty TV newscasters say something like: "If you're interested in the weather, it will rain tomorrow"? And if you're not interested in the weather, will it snow? In this case, the newscaster can assume that his or her audience is interested. (If it isn't interested, why even mention the topic?)

Other such empty introductions include:

- For your information . . .
- In case you were wondering . . .
- The facts are these:

In that latter case, you're telling readers that facts are about to follow, and then you follow with facts. Isn't that good? Isn't that, in a sense, following the hoary advice of "Tell 'em what you're going to tell 'em; tell 'em; tell 'em what you just told 'em"? It is that, indeed, but I don't necessarily agree that it's *good* advice. Avoid telling readers what you're going to tell them—just tell them.

Throat-clearing leads. And, especially, the pronouncement lead. For example:

> Police are still trying to figure out how it happened.
> A robber managed to steal a 37-ton safe from a valve manufacturer's office Thursday night, without a trace.

At best, this lead is a part of the story but not the important part. Sneaking out with thirty-seven tons in tow is the real story. At worst, the lead is the work of a lazy writer looking to surprise us with a chitchatty statement—a pronouncement, if you will—instead of letting the writing do the work.

The one-word lead, which on the surface seems to be the epitome in concision, is almost always pure waste of space. For example:

> Taxes.
> Just the word makes people shudder.

This is not just uninformative. It's also dull. Or how about some other pronouncement leads:

> It's an old story . . .
> It's another tale of man bites dog.
> It was a dark and stormy night.

Perhaps one of the most common superfluous leads is the one that spends a couple of paragraphs setting the scene. In fiction, description delays the story. In nonfiction, the danger is larger. The story is delayed, yes, but it seems that some writers think the description *is* the story. People are the story. What's more, scene-setting in nonfiction is self-indulgence — perhaps more accurately, self-consciousness. "Look at me! I'm reporting!" it seems to say, especially if you place yourself in that scene. Here's an extreme example from a writer who should know better — me. Here's the lead to an article I once wrote about professionalism in writing:

> Let's imagine for a moment an anthropomorphized *Titanic*, with cute little smiley face on the bow, kind of like Tuggy the Tugboat in the children's books. Now, imagine what the *Titanic* must have tried to say to the iceberg coming out of the dark before it finally bore down and ripped out ol' unsinkable's guts. Well, if you can't imagine it, I can, and I can empathize with the *Titanic*, because I once told a roomful of writers that they sometimes could expect no more from editors than used-car dealers could expect from their customers.

My editor wisely slashed the first sentence and started the piece with "Try to imagine what the *Titanic* . . ." Imagining the anthropomorphized *Titanic* was abstract scene-setting; I was setting up an image that was self-indulgent and, most important, unneeded. In doing so, I was delaying my point.

Empty transitions and connections. From a news report on rising crime rates: "Jane Doe is installing a home security system. And she's not the only one. Thousands of people in the tri-state area will buy such systems this year."

"And she's not the only one" is not only fatuous (if she *were* the only one, the home security business would be a little pale), but also unnecessary. Remove it, and the connection remains clear. "Jane Doe is installing a home security system. Thousands of people in the tri-state area will buy such systems this year." Better yet, to stress that the facts are related, draw them into the same sentence. "Jane Doe is installing a home security system, as will thousands of people in the tri-state area this year."

Another example, from that doomed *Titanic* article: I told of a request from one of my writers for an advance on her advance, which she needed to fix her word processor. I explained why, corporately, it was so difficult to grant that request. Then: "Still, two hours later, enough money to cover the monitor was on its way . . . and I'm glad I could help. This doesn't precisely nominate me for Mother Teresa's successor, however."

I look at those sentences now, and wonder why I tagged the second with "however." The context of that sentence clearly indicates contrast. "However" is superfluous.

"Well" is a pesky transition word—again, one that I overuse (I used it, I'm sure you noticed, in the *Titanic* lead). Writers often use it as a timing element, to communicate, "Well, I've thought about that. . ." Which means the author is intruding. For example, "Some observers propose that the U.S. revamp its education funding policies. Well, there's some advantage to that, but. . ."

Here, "well" introduces the potential for further intrusion—it's an open sesame word that can lead to personal comment that may not be appropriate to what you're writing.

Other phrases and words to watch for include "So, as you see . . ." or, more briefly, "So, . . ." Or, more verbosely, "As you can plainly see . . ."

Beware, too, of transitions and connections that lead the reader by the proverbial nose through the manuscript. Consider this example: "I gave in to the demands. Why? you might ask. Because I had no other choice." That intrusive "Why? you might ask" drags the reader from the first sentence to the third. Better to make it just one sentence: "I gave in to the demands because I had no other choice." Better yet: "Having no other choice, I gave in to the demands."

Empty summation. At the end of a series of instructions or procedures trails "A complex process that must be followed carefully." Or appended to the adventures of a mischievous cat in a children's story: "All in all, quite a day." If you've communicated the complexity of the process you're describing, if your tale of the mischievous cat has given the readers a sense of adventure, such tags are superfluous. If they aren't, if they're needed to communicate what's been going on, your story needs revising, not recapping. I point to editor/writer/ teacher Don McKinney, who once ended an article on magazine writing this way: "To sum things up, I won't sum things up. That part of an article always bores me. If you're not sure you know what I said, go back and read it again."

Empty reaction. Oh? And what is empty reaction? Meaningless words of response, repetitions, questions that do little more than bridge or prod, and other fill best left to polite conversations than to prose. I discovered the value of chopping empty reaction when I was copyediting question-and-answer interviews for *Writer's Digest.* You know the type:

> **Question:** How did you get interested in writing?
> **Answer:** My mother inspired me.
> **Question:** That happens a lot.
> **Answer:** She always had books around me, and would read me wonderful tales before I went to bed . . .

The interviewer's reaction, "That happens a lot," adds not a whit to the story. We would edit the interview so that it would read:

> **Question:** How did you get started in writing?
> **Answer:** My mother inspired me. She always had books around me, and would . . .

Savings: six words, if you look at it on the small scale, but on a larger scale, at least a couple of valuable magazine column lines.

Later, I found this to be an equally effective trimming tool when writing radio scripts and dialogue in fiction:

> "Your time is up, Gertrude," John said.
> "Oh? And why is that?"
> "The clock just ran out."

Carefully consider "Oh? And why is that?" Is it necessary? Can it be cut, so that John simply says "Your time is up, Gertrude. The clock just ran out"?

Worse yet is empty reaction that comes not from people in your stories, but from *you.* Such author-driven reaction often comes in the form of rhetorical questions: "How did Paul Bunyan chop down the forest?" The reader tends to respond with such rhetorically questioning answers as, "What, you expect *me* to answer? *You* are writing this." Don't ask the question. Just give the answer. Author-driven reaction also takes the form of unneeded self-prods, transitions and introductions, such as the "Oh? And what is empty reaction?" that began this section.

As with everything else we might consider wordy, we evaluate whether supposedly empty reactions have other, less obvious functions. Perhaps, in a short story, you need such reaction for pacing, or to bring verisimilitude to a piece of dialogue. Perhaps the reader will expect reaction — even if it's a simple dumbfounded repetition after a surprising revelation ("He's your *father*?"). After all, conversation rarely consists of two people swapping soliloquies, so passages of dialogue, especially long ones, must be punctuated by reaction and response to feel realistic. It's better if reaction and response move the plot, or add to characterization, or perform some function other than providing pacing filler.

Tangential material. Asides, by-the-ways, interesting parenthetical thoughts that have nothing to do with the core of the manuscript — these are the tangents that can sidetrack you, divert your readers' attention, and add fat to your words. It's filler. (Did you know that some twenty-five *hundred* publications buy fillers from freelance writers? It's a great market.) For instance, what does that parenthetical thought about fillers have to do with anything? Yes, the information applies to you, since you're a writer. And you just might find it interesting, even valuable. But it has nothing to do with what I'm writing here (other than serving as example, of course).

Empty comments on what the manuscript does *not* deliver. How many celebrity "interviews" have you read that essentially covered nothing more than how hard it was to get the interview? Thirty paragraphs of some surly star or reclusive writer saying "I don't want to talk to you" and slamming the door. That's thirty perhaps eloquent paragraphs of the author saying, "I didn't come up with anything, and here's why." That's thirty paragraphs of apologies.

How many speeches have you attended in which the speaker said, "I meant to show you a chart, but I didn't have time to put it together"? It would have taken only a little more time to delete that apology from the speech.

How many articles have you read in which the writer tells you, "Solving the problems of the universe is beyond the scope of this article"? If you have written the article well, its focus (and what is outside of it) shouldn't have to be stated directly.

Yes, explain the absence of something the reader might expect to see in your manuscript (for example, "Mr. Howard, the administrator in charge of the department accused of the misappropriations, was unavailable for comment"). But the ultimate way to communicate that you came up with nothing to tell us is to tell us nothing.

4. The Evasive (Intentional or Otherwise)

Don't quote me on this, but evasive language has been known to hurt communication for the most part.

Just what the heck am I dodging in that sentence, other than the responsibility of having said it? Evasive language hurts communication. Period. No quibbling, no ducking, no hiding behind qualifiers and maybes and ifs and "gosh don't hit me if you disagree."

Evasion, wordy and corrosive, includes:

Qualifiers. Many of the empty qualifiers I discussed above—*generally, usually, basically* and the like—are most often used as tools of evasion. As an editor, I'm as guilty of using qualifiers as anyone, especially in writing letters to authors. "I'm returning your book because it's a bit unusual" is softer than "I'm returning your book because it's unusual" (which is in turn softer than "I didn't like it").

There's a place for qualifiers, and sometimes that place is in your sentences. If you can't screw up the courage to say, "Your plan is impossible," saying, "Your plan is *a bit* impossible" fairly shouts your cowardice.

Apologies and indecisive waffling. For example, *"I could be wrong about this, but I think* New York City is in New York state." But don't quote me on that.

The danger here surpasses the simple weak and wordy waffle. There's the problem of sloppy research, pure and simple. If you could be wrong, *do your research until you know you are right*. Double-check. The stomach flu hit President Bush on a tour of Japan in early 1992; he collapsed at a state dinner. Not long after, someone called CNN pretending to be Bush's doctor and told CNN that the President was dead. For some bizarre reason, someone handed the item to an anchor, who started to read the "news." Luckily, someone stopped him. But before he was stopped, the anchor, in one of the grandest displays of journalistic malpractice I've ever heard of, said, "I say right off the bat, we have not confirmed this through any other source...." On a more innocuous scale, "I could be wrong about this, but..."

Do your research; be sure, so you don't have to waste words — and tax reader credibility — with apologies.

Euphemisms and dodge words. "You have procured a zero reduction of billable hours" instead of "You're fired" sounds like a ridiculous, made-up example, because it is. But how about a ridiculous real example? One company euphemized layoffs as "indefinite idling."

"Aesthetic" evasion. This includes hiding meanings in poetry, working to obscure rather than clarify in "literary" prose. In my brief short-story contest-judging days, I saw my share of manuscripts that lead off with some shadowy "he" doing this and that. We find out later who he is. This isn't so much a physical length problem as it as a mental length problem. You have the reader wondering instead of reading. This is neither suspense nor art.

"Um" words. That is, words that, like "um" in speech, are used to hesitate and delay. They, um, *basically* signal lack of confidence.

Invasion of the Evasion

Evasion has its place, of course. We're a polite society (for the most part, he said evasively). There's no point, for instance, in my saying to an author I'm working with, "Those first six paragraphs are pure tangential deadwood," when I can say, "I think the manuscript takes a bit long in getting started," and get the same results.

If you feel you must evade, do it just once in a sentence. Don't write, "I think Smith may be the best to play shortstop ever." "Smith may be the best" and "I think Smith is the best" say slightly different things with the same philosophy: The writer is hedging.

Worse Yet

Closely related to "the evasive" are "the misleading" and "the deceptive" — evasions to the point of misdirection, to the point of lying. This is a big topic, one I could spend page upon page discussing. But because misleading and lying are matters of honesty and intention more than of concision and clarity, I will condense my advice to this: Don't do it. If you're prone to twisting words to place incorrect ideas and impressions in readers' minds, you need a book on ethics and not one on writing skills.

5. The Weak-Kneed and the Passive

Back to Nintendo: My four-year-old once delighted in watching his brother play video games in the living room, then running into the kitchen to tell me how the games were going. "You have to run away from the ogre," he'd tell me with four-year-old earnestness, "or you'll get dead."

I love that phrase. You don't die; you get dead. You acquire a state of deadness. You get deadness the way you get letters in the mail. It's a gentle, almost euphemistic way of saying, hey, it's only a game, and you don't really "die" when you lose a "life." You aren't killed. You passively cease to exist.

But at the keyboard, I am not a four-year-old, nor are my readers a collective adoring father willing not only to overlook puffed-up and lame language, but also to delight in it. If I persist in peppering my prose with softening passives, like "get" in "get dead," their ignoring my prose won't make it dead. It will simply kill it.

Various verbs can achieve similar weak-kneed emptiness. For example, "choose" in "I chose to ignore him." This not only is weaker, but also emphasizes the choosing over what was chosen. "I ignored him" is more to the point. Let's watch some of these other verbs at, um, "work":

Arrive. "We arrived at a decision" becomes "We decided."

Attain. "The West High team attained the championship" becomes "The West High team won the championship."

Be. "I'll be meeting with the committee tomorrow" becomes "I meet with the committee tomorrow."

Come. "The car came to a stop" becomes "The car stopped"; "I came across a new way of preparing my tax return" becomes "I discovered a new way of preparing my tax return."

Contribute. "I contributed my suggestion to cut expenses" becomes "I suggested cutting expenses."

Do. "Let's do lunch" becomes obsolete.

Gain. "We all want to gain success" becomes "We all want to succeed."

Get. "Get going" becomes "Go."

Give. "Give your writing energy" becomes "Energize your writing."

Go. "I went to lunch" becomes "I lunched."

Have. "You have your fate in control" becomes "You control your fate."

Hold. "We held a conversation" becomes "We conversed." (Better yet, "We talked.")

Make. "She made reference to the first-quarter report" becomes "She referred to the first-quarter report."

Offer. "I offered my appraisal of the situation" becomes "I appraised the situation."

Pay. "Pay heed to the warning" becomes "Heed the warning."

Perform. "He performed an operation on the patient" becomes "He operated on the patient."

Place. "Place him under detention" becomes "Detain him."

Proceed. "I proceeded to eat my lunch" becomes "I ate my lunch."

Provide. "The city provides street-cleaning services" becomes "The city cleans the streets."

Put. "We put the machinery to the test" becomes "We tested the machinery."

Reach. "We reached a compromise" becomes "We compromised."

Take. "I took a shower" becomes "I showered."

When you spot such potentially empty verbs, scan the rest of the sentence for another verb. In "The city provides street-cleaning services," we spot "provides" and scan to find "clean," though it's been disguised as a noun ("cleaning"). The second verb you find is often stronger; if so, that one should propel your sentence. (I further discuss verb-into-noun conversions as a warning signal of wordiness on page 113.)

Don't go overboard in eliminating these words, as often they perform legitimate functions. "Perform" performs appropriately in the previous sentence. You could, I suppose, trim it back to read "they function legitimately," but performing legitimate functions and functioning legitimately sound to me like two different things.

Hidden Weaknesses

Some writers avoid "is" and its conjugations with two verbs with vaguely greater power but still decidedly weak: "stand" and "sit." For example: "The man sat twiddling his fingers." What's important in that sentence? Sitting? Or twiddling? Better is "The man twiddled his fingers."

Or how about this: "John stood there glaring at me." "Stood there" is a slightly more active version of "was." Instead, write "John glared at me."

But here, too, there will be exceptions. Don't delete "stood there" in the example about John if you're trying to show continuity, and "glaring," continuous, is more appropriate than "glared," one-time action.

You can also weaken sentences by casting them into less active verb tenses. For instance:

Check your will. Often, casting a sentence in the future tense will make it wordy and will dilute its impact. For example, take the sentence that preceded this one. Convert it to the present tense, and gain power: "Often, casting a sentence in the future tense makes it wordy and dilutes its impact." (However, don't convert the future tense into the present if the future tense is truly needed. "If you cast a sentence in the future tense, you will make it wordy. If you don't, you won't." The difference between that example and the first one is the word "if," which casts the sentence in the true future tense—the first example is in a modified present tense.)

There are times when removing the will from a true future tense construction infuses a sentence with power. "Touch my chocolate chip cookies and you die" has more impact than "Touch my chocolate chip cookies and you will die."

Eliminate the "deadwould." That's what Joe Floren in *Write Smarter, Not Harder* calls the often unnecessary "would." "I would agree with you." You would? Under what circumstances? "I agree with you" does the job—unless you mean something like "I would agree with you if you were right."

It's sometimes better to be a "have not" than a "have." Sometimes "have" can be eliminated by casting the sentence in the past tense instead of the past perfect. "I have made my bed" communicates little more than "I made my bed" does. "We have eaten breakfast and have gone to the store" doesn't tell us anything different from "We ate breakfast and went to the store."

6. The Weak, the Noncommittal and the Hesitant

Weak writing is meek writing, more timid than evasive. In college, for instance, I told my girlfriend that I was in love with her. She bristled. The passive phrasing, she told me sternly (herself a word person), meant I was hedging—even if unconsciously. My expression of love was weak, uncommitted, she contended.

I didn't marry this person. Maybe she was right. Maybe I was only "in love." (Maybe I was irritated that she couldn't take what I said in the spirit in which it was intended.) The point is that saying "I love you" is stronger, more forceful than the weak-minded "I'm in love with you." The latter has the rhythm and the feel of "I'm in Kansas City with you."

Therefore, I'm in favor of trimming sentences.

Better yet, I favor trimming sentences.

Related to the weak and noncommittal is the hesitant, words that either delay what you're about to say or that under the surface signal that what follows isn't particularly pleasant. For instance, such introductory phrases as "To be honest" or "To be perfectly frank" might be viewed as empty introductions, stating the already understood. Why would anyone write "To be honest," when they would never introduce a sentence with the opposite: "To be dishonest? . . ." But such phrases aren't precisely empty. They tell the reader/listener, "Gee, I know what I'm saying might seem a little blunt, and I understand that, but I'm going to give it to you straight." There's a place for that, I suppose, but when shooting from the hip, hesitating before drawing can be deadly. To be frank. A hesitation isn't quite a waffle, isn't quite an evasion, but it *is* longer than necessary.

I wrote in an early draft of this chapter this sentence: "Familiarize yourself as best you can with the enemy." The phrase "as best you can" is, again, not quite a waffle, not quite an evasion. It's me saying, "Well, I realize you might think it's a bit of work, and I don't want to force you, but maybe you should think about it. . . ."

7. The Affected

Affected writing is closely related to euphemistic writing, though this time the writer has something to show off instead of something to hide. But pretension is no more acceptable to readers than evasion, so it is my goal to demonstrate the considered correlation between movement toward actualization of pomposity and vocalization of same and the recession of verbal meaning. Or to put it in English . . . if you want to sound pompous, you do it at the expense of communication.

Affectations generally travel in packs. A writer prone to the haughty word, for instance, is usually prone to a lot of haughty words, leading to haughty sentences, paragraphs and entire manuscripts.

But they can also slip in unescorted, in some of the most unlikely places. One day I was listening to an oldies radio station. Previewing the next DJ's program, the announcer said, "Stacy will actuate another eighteen tunes in a row for you." *Actuate?* Why not "start," or "play"? "Actuate" is out of character with a station that speaks informally of "tunes," especially since actuating songs sounds like something either robots or accountants would do. Besides, I'm listening to the station for old songs, not new gobbledyspeak. In this case, the affectation isn't muddy so much as it is jarring. Muddy or jarring, it's longer than it has to be.

Stick to the workhorses and avoid these high horses:

The haughty, the snooty and the pretentious. Let's call this "The Overly Formal, Part I." This is writing that elevates itself above its audience, turning that writing garret into the ivory tower. Food writing, the Calvin Trillins aside, seems wrought with such pretension, as if the writer is convincing us that a mouth that can utter superior vocabulary must also be blessed by the requisite superior pallet. *Roadfood* is Michael and Jane Stern's directory of great down-home roadside dining across America—the meatloaf and gravy places. The book and the writing within are marvelously down-home. But a *USA Weekend* writer, reviewing *Roadfood*, mentioned an Albuquerque barbeque joint listed in the book and suggested the "sweet potato pie for the perfect denouement" (a phrase the Sterns thankfully did not use). I can picture the waitress now: "Hey, Harley! Two Adam and Eves on a raft, java light and a slice of perfect denouement!" Writing about meat and potatoes shouldn't be adorned with caviar words.

Included here are such things as using the editorial we, "shall" instead of "will," and pretzeling sentences to keep them from ending with prepositions—ending a sentence with a preposition is better than filling it with a pretension, so let's say "I wonder who she'll go with," unless the formal version is dictated by the tone and diction of the manuscript (a stiff character in a novel saying it, for instance).

Pretension results from a variety of motivations. To establish superiority over the audience is one. But much pretension isn't so cynically inspired. Some of it, frankly, just happens. Spontaneous elevation. Some of it results not so much from writers' deflated view of the readers as it does from their inflated view of writers. Not of themselves as writers. But of writers and what writers do in general. These are the folks who believe that being a writer is a lofty calling (it is) and that the words writers use must have similar loft (they don't). I like what Don McKinney said about that problem: "Don't write like a writer—just write."

All the above are also traps of a closely related problem:

The pretty. This is "The Overly Formal, Part II," and it differs from "the haughty, the snooty and the pretentious" only in intent. It results not from disdain for the reader, but from a sort of politeness toward the reader (not to mention an inflated sense of what Writers, with quill pen and smoking jacket, are supposed to do). Whatever the source, pretty grammar leads to both physical and mental length. "I wonder with whom she will go" is a perfectly grammatical sentence, but it's pretty stiff.

One of the dangers of pretty grammar is that it is so far from the familiar that you can trip over it, as a sportscaster did recently. "Nuxhall will take part in Reds Baseball Fantasy Week, of which he has been part of."

And then there's the worst pretty grammar of all: pretty, and wrong. "I wonder whom she will pick"; "Tom gave a present to my husband and I." In the first sentence, "who" is correct; in the second, "me" instead of "I." Either way, pretty grammar has made the sentences stiffer and verbose.

The professionally confusing. Read, "jargon"—used when jargon isn't necessary. For example: Talk about your insult to injury; not only am I on the verge of suffering from male pattern baldness, but now I have to *say* it, too. When I was growing up, men were bald. But apparently they felt that mere baldness didn't evoke enough sympathy, so they invented the much more horrific-sounding male pattern baldness. But since women rarely lose their hair, why do we need all those extra words? What other kind of baldness is there? Eagle pattern baldness?

The professionally confusing varies from profession to profession, and includes such gems as *the military* ("anti-personnel projectile" instead of bullet, "eliminate with extreme prejudice" instead of kill, eight-hundred-dollar "directed impact propulsion devices" instead of seven-dollar hammers), *the legal* ("and/or," "pursuant to," "herewith," "heretofore"), *the academic* ("learning facilitators" instead of teachers, children with "attention deficit disorders" instead of class clowns, "physical and life enhancement studies" instead of gym class), *the governmental* ("revenue enhancements" instead of taxes, "soft wheel infrastructure systems" instead of roads, every other word in any tax form), *the business/corporate* ("negative growth" instead of recession, "rightsizing" instead of layoffs, "field service representatives" instead of repairmen, "previously owned vehicles" instead of used cars) and other insular, evasive pomposities designed as much to confuse and impress as they are to espouse the philosophy of another bit of jargon: CYA. ("Cover Your...umm, Behind.")

These locutions are bad enough when they stay within the bounds of the professions that created or adopted them. But when they slip out to the general public, so that your memo about the company picnic is dotted with heretofores, or your nonfiction book about making kites is dropping ibids and footnotes about, you're in trouble. Extreme examples, but ones I've seen, though I've disguised them slightly to protect the verbose. Here's one I haven't disguised: A house layout printed in the "homes for sale" section of a recent newspaper featured a "welcome room" instead of a foyer, and a "motor room" instead of the garage.

The danger of using the professionally confusing lies not only in the words but in the writing style. Such affectations lead to stiff, formal, saluting, stone cold writing that's just as loose as a Buckingham Palace guard and usually as communicative. Such writing is often rife with other problems outlined in this chapter: passives, evasions, prolixities, overkill and other false steps that "elevate" the writer and distance him or her from the reader.

The humble. For some reason, many people believe that the innocuous word "me" is somehow evil. To avoid "me," they will say, "He spoke to John and I." Worse yet, "He spoke to John and myself." This might result as much from not wanting to sound selfish ("me," often associated with the self-centeredness of childhood, communicates concentration on self more than the more adult "I") as it does from misguided shots at "proper" grammar. "He spoke to myself" might result from the syndrome that gives us "This writer believes . . ." instead of "I believe." Whatever the cause, writers such as yourself should listen to myself and use "me" where appropriate. There are also elements of "pretty grammar" and "the self-indulgent" in this "myself" business.

The faddish. Like hula hoops, faddish words and phrases come and go. When they're popular, they spin aimlessly about. You can have fun with hula hoop words; just don't take them to work with you.

For instance, "people" seems to have fallen out of favor in certain circles, replaced by the more faddish "persons" or "individuals," as in "That day we interviewed 117 individuals." "People" would work more efficiently, unless you want to emphasize how grueling it was to conduct 117 distinct, time-consuming, seemingly endless interviews. Or if you want to stress the parts of the group rather than the group itself: "We aren't dealing with *people*," said the social worker. "We're dealing with *individuals*."

Worse yet is something like "I spoke with seven *individual people*." "I spoke with seven people" will do.

"At this point in time" instead of "now" was all the rage for a time. So were Pet Rocks. More recently, I've seen—yes, in print— such locutions as "He's going to step down from office—*NOT!*" How nice that we're learning the elements of subtle writing not from Strunk and White but from Strunk and Wayne's World.

Can you get away with such faddishness? In the short run, perhaps, but doubtful. In the long run? I don't think so! And here's why: Someone reading this paragraph over my shoulder as I write it probably wouldn't pause at "I don't think so!" It's a popular catch-phrase now (quickly being supplanted by *NOT!*, however), and is fairly invisible. However, you're reading this book far into my future— at least fourteen months from now. In my future, in your now, "I don't think so!" is sounding pretty dusty, isn't it? (And if you don't remember Wayne's World by the time these words reach you, you see my point.)

The overly delicate. Delicacy has its place. "Passing on" is often more gently appropriate than "dying." But don't write about John Kennedy "passing on" in 1963. It's too gentle for not just a death but an assassination. Worse yet, perhaps, it's mushily vague.

Much of this depends on context. "Sanitation engineer" on a job description is delicate, but appropriately so. Writing that your hard-boiled detective is searching a surveillance subject's trash in the early morning before the sanitation engineers clear it away is silly.

The politically correct. I believe that the term "spousal unit" replacing "husband," "wife" or "spouse" started as a joke, but it unfortunately has been adapted for occasional serious use. I once heard someone refer to his wife as his "partner in life" because, he claimed, the phrase "my wife" communicated ownership. His "partner in life" was not his slave, his property. Fine. But the word "my" communicates relationship as often as it does ownership. My kids refer to the house I'm typing these words in the same way I do, as "my house"— even though my name is on the mortgage (and even though the bank really owns it anyway). I refer to the Cincinnati Reds as my team, even though the closest thing I'll have to ownership is renting a couple of seats at the stadium for a few hours at a stretch.

The politically correct is different from but similar to the overly delicate, in that politically correct speech seeks to avoid categorizing, stereotyping or insensitively labeling people or situations. Noble goals. But let's not go overboard. I once knew an editor who wanted to edit the phrase "colored paper" (as in "Don't type a manuscript on colored paper") out of a manuscript. "Hued paper" is the phrase he wanted to use. OK, it's shorter. It's also political correctness gone wild.

The restaurants that always give me heartburn are restaurants with "waitpersons." Let's not deform and balloon the language in our efforts to achieve linguistic sexual equality. I've heard "waitperson" stretched into further illogical extreme: "member of the waitstaff."

Why can't all people who wait tables be waiters? One who waits is a waiter. One who writes is a writer, and not a writeperson. (And heaven knows, one who writes is not a writress, despite the appalling but thankfully archaic use of words like "poetess" and "songstress"). It takes a little regearing of the mind to accept a woman, for so long referred to as a waitress, as a waiter. But far less regearing than to accept this *waitperson*, this new firework of a word, lengthy and unusual and more than a little silly.

Don't get me wrong. I favor eliminating sexist attitudes and sexist phrasings, just as I favor accurate and nonjudgmental ways to refer to people and situations. Yet I also believe that: 1) Language follows thought, and not vice versa—let's change the attitudes first. 2) There are better solutions to sexism and other prejudice in language problems than applying the dictates, not to mention the length, of agenda-specific Newspeak bureaucratese.

8. The Circuitous

Winding, twisting sentences add words to and leech understandability from your writing. Circuitous writing is a symptom of not presenting information in a crisp order appropriate to the subject at hand. "When starting your car, turn the ignition, put the car into gear, and go. Be sure, though, that you have inserted the key into the ignition before you turn it." An extreme example, but one that will demonstrate how presenting information in proper order—whether that order uses chronology, importance of information, whatever—will allow you to present it more compactly.

This has a smaller side, as well. Why say, "Pick up the folder that is green" when you can say "Pick up the green folder"?

To avoid prolixity:

Draw related words together. Roundabout writing often puts distance between subject and verb, verb and object, adverb and verb, adjective and noun. In the above example, the modifier "green" has been separated from what it is modifying, "folder." Sometimes modifiers can even be found in different sentences. "I chose the car. It was the blue one." Those sentences can be compressed into one: "I chose the blue car."

Sometimes important related words are not misplaced but misused; they aren't modifying anything. In a draft of this book, I wrote: "To reduce the potential for becoming self-conscious about your writing..." In that sentence, "self-conscious" is a hidden modifier more efficiently used if it were allowed to modify something. To use it more effectively, I subconsciously asked a question of the sentence. If you become self-conscious about your writing, what do you end up with? Self-conscious writing. Compress the becoming part out of it, and convert what you're becoming into an adjective, and you come up with a wording that I eventually used: "To reduce the potential for self-conscious writing..."

And on page 27, I discuss what the reader understands about the physical world: The first draft contained this paragraph:

The cartoon is labeled "Beginning Food Critic." In it, a writer sits at a restaurant table, his right hand wrist-deep in a bowl while with his left he jots onto a notepad: "The bisque, though a bit hot, was sufficiently deep and wet." That's from cartoonist John Caldwell.

Here I've devoted a sentence to identifying the cartoonist, when I can use the name as an adjective: "A John Caldwell cartoon." I've also made two references to the cartoon—one directly as "The cartoon," and the other as "it." I replaced the pronoun with the noun, reworked the sentence slightly, and came up with:

In a John Caldwell cartoon labeled "Beginning Food Critic," a writer sits at a restaurant table, his right hand wrist-deep in a bowl while with his left he jots onto a notepad: "The bisque, though a bit hot, was sufficiently deep and wet."

Beware the "Noun is a noun who/that/which verbs" construction. For example, "John is a manager who cares." To remove this type of roundaboutness, compress the two nouns into one or the other—usually the first, the subject noun. Then drop the weak verb and the reflexive pronoun ("who"), and use the verb in the tag phrase to drive the entire sentence.

Using the example sentence, we compress the noun "manager" into the subject noun, "John," drop "who" and "is" and let "cares" drive the sentence. "John cares."

Now, "manager" might have to stay in, depending on the context and your goals. Perhaps you're writing about uncaring managers, and you want to stress that John is the exception. "John is a manager who cares." But if we've had proper introduction to John and we know he's a manager, "John cares" will make the point. Perhaps we've not even met John; we can still introduce him properly so we don't have to resort to the "noun is a noun" construction. "Not all managers are so insensitive. John cares."

Another common and irksome construction: "The noun was an adjective one." For example, "The first attempt was a successful one." Compress "one" into "attempt": "The first attempt was successful." Better yet: "The first attempt succeeded."

Identify the key words in the sentence. In "Pick up the green folder," the subject is important, but understood: "you." The verb is important: "pick up." The object of the verb is important: "folder." The color of the folder is important in identifying which folder: "green."

Now, align them. Bang bang bang. Pick up/folder/green.

Finally, create a sentence of them. Pick up the folder green. Does it make sense? Revise it, touch it up. Pick up the green folder. This can lead to some robotic writing: subject verb object. But it can also help you identify the core of the sentence.

Pay attention to long sentences. What do I mean by long? "Pick up the folder that is green" is long mentally, though not physically. You're looking for mental as well as physical length, but I'll grant you that physical length is easier to spot. Here's a whopper of a sentence I wrote in the first draft of this chapter: "If you cover history as background in the first couple of pages, then return to it near the middle of the manuscript, then allow a little more of the rise to power to slip in near the end, you're very likely repeating if not significant information, then at least setup information—the information needed to establish three separate sections of the manuscript as history." Sixty-five words. I didn't count them to realize I needed to trim that one back; I just paid attention to my yearning for an intermission somewhere near the middle of the sentence so I could go to the bathroom. I broke the sentence into more easily handled units.

Get to the point. I'm tiring of the practice of writers making announcements before telling us anything. "A decision should come tomorrow. Congress will decide whether to reveal a full list of representatives who wrote bad checks on the Federal bank." We the readers know that a decision is coming long before we know what people are deciding. Get to the point. "Congress will decide tomorrow whether . . ."

Don't back into your point with negatives; make it directly. This is a little like expressing the first number as -1×-1 instead of more simply as 1. For example: The phrase "When appropriate, don't use negatives" can be more succinctly written as "When appropriate, use positives," by stripping the "not" out and twisting negative to positive. This switching has three advantages: It's shorter, it's more direct, and it leaves less opportunity for confusion, especially that caused by using double negatives, such as "The plan is not without its disadvantages." Huh? Does this mean it has advantages, or what? (Speaking of potential for confusion, I once knew a writer who used "The situation is not indifferent from what it was" to mean that "The situation is the same as it was.")

One grammar book suggests that "some negatives allow almost formulaic translations into affirmatives," and gives several examples, among them:

- "Not many" becomes "few"
- "Not the same" becomes "different"
- "Not old enough" becomes "too young"
- "Not possible" becomes "impossible"

OK, I'll buy those examples to a point, but other examples on the list include:

- "Does not have" becomes "lacks"
- "Did not consider" becomes "ignored"
- "Not certain" becomes "uncertain"
- "Did not" becomes "failed to"

Well, *maybe*, if you really mean your house *lacks* termites instead of your house *does not have* termites. Absence of termites is hardly a lack. "I did not consider your feelings" and "I ignored your feelings" are vastly different concepts. "Uncertain" is a condition; "not certain" might mean I simply haven't yet decided. And the fact that I did not run anyone over with my car on the way to work this morning doesn't mean that I failed to run anyone down.

Still, the technique, used appropriately, can reduce prolixity. "You won't be paid unless you turn in a time card" is circuitous; better is "To be paid, you must turn in a time card."

9. The Self-Indulgent

One of the lengthiest, bulkiest, most cumbersome words is the seemingly sleek *I*, which populates many manuscripts the way dust bunnies populate the spaces under beds.

In today's newspaper, for instance, one story began: "I remember the Friday afternoon I first made the acquaintance of Tony." How nice. Is this a story about the author, a personal essay? No. It's a roundup article listing the various Cincinnati ethnic groceries, one of which Tony runs. So why is the first word we read *I?* Why is the first character we meet *I?* Why is *I* standing in the way of what readers want to see? I want to ask this writer to get out of my way in the same way that I ask my six-year-old to stop standing in front of the TV. So this particular lead is not only wasting space, but also misdirecting the reader.

There are other problems with this lead, most related to the self-indulgences of the writer. "I remember the Friday afternoon . . ." That's news? That's what readers would find interesting or important — remembering? And of course the writer remembers it — if he didn't, how could he write about it? "I first made the acquaintance." Two problems here. 1) How many times can you make someone's acquaintance? Seems like there's *only* a first time, so the "first" can go from that sentence. And 2) "made the acquaintance" is too flowery a phrasing, too self-consciously "literate" for an informational piece, when just meeting Tony would have sufficed.

So why am I telling you this in the first person? Why aren't I taking my own advice? Well, there are times, I contend, when writing nonfiction in the first person is good:

1. When you are establishing a rapport with the reader (as I'm trying to do here).
2. When you are the authority.
3. When the reader indeed cares about you.
4. When you are indeed the true subject of the material (as in personal essays).
5. When you're letting the reader know that your manuscript isn't speaking from an objective viewpoint, that what you're describing is filtered through your subjective viewpoint.

To avoid allowing yourself to barge into your writing:

Avoid the first person unless you are truly part of the story, or, in the case of fiction, the first person truly fulfills your storytelling needs. The first person not only introduces greater length to a manuscript, but introduces another "character" the reader must keep track of. When you do use the first person, use it confidently and boldly. Do your part to hasten the death of a decades-dusty journalistic affectation that this writer disdains and that this writer has mentioned before—and that's using "this writer" instead of "I." Yes, the purpose of the phrase is ostensibly to allow the writer to step out of the way, to distance writer and story. Admirable, but futile. "This writer" is distracting in its pretension, just as it is when athletes or entertainers refer to themselves in the third person.

Avoid subtler but equally distracting author intrusions. That's a good idea, don't you agree? Well, avoiding author intrusions *is* a good idea, but my stepping in to ask that question was more than just unnecessary. By asking it, I was making my presence obvious; I was bursting through the page out at the reader as abruptly and alarmingly as a circus tiger through a paper hoop.

From a horror novel by an author whose work I otherwise respect: "But it was, of course, too late."

"Of course"? Who decided that it was, of course, too late? A character in the novel? No. The author. More than just two words have dropped into the equally communicative sentence "But it was too late"—the author's clumsy two feet have dropped in as well. (Even clumsier, by the way, is the labored "as a matter of course.")

Such author intrusion is unnecessary and damaging. By saying, "That's a good idea, don't you agree?", I've chosen to do some of your thinking for you. That's condescension. By saying "of course" it was too late, the author is saying, "Sure, I knew that all along. I told you so." It adds a smarmy element to the sentence. That, too, is condescension.

Avoid talking about things only you care about. Self-indulgence can commandeer small sections of a manuscript, and it can commandeer entire manuscripts, as it does with the intensely personal stories I described in chapter one. With rare exception, readers do not care about you. On one level, they care about the subject of your manuscript. On a deeper level, they care about themselves. Tell them about the topic, and ultimately about themselves, and they listen. Tell them about you with no explication of either the topic or the reader, and they turn the page.

Keep your opinion to yourself. I once wrote a business memo describing a book I wanted to publish. To describe its unusual nature, I wrote, "If I were a Hollywood ad writer, I'd call this book *Writer's Market Meets the Writer's Essential Desk Reference Meets The Song-*

writer's and Musician's Guide to Nashville, starring Gene Hackman (because Gene Hackman stars in everything these days)." I committed two fouls here—one, injecting my sense of humor into an otherwise straightforward memo. How large a foul is open to debate; a touch of humor here and there, even in a business environment, is sometimes appropriate—especially if the audience knows something about the personality of the speaker. The second foul was more serious: my injecting my opinion that Gene Hackman appears in too many movies. Humor or not, who cares other than me and possibly Gene Hackman?

That's not egregious, certainly. Egregious is something I saw in a book on characterization in fiction: "Only idiots champion public transport." Agree or disagree, what does it have to do with writing fiction?

Especially beware parentheses. Opinion often slips into a manuscript shielded by parentheses.

I will mention but briefly that opinion shouldn't color objective reporting. The danger of writing nonfiction tainted by personal bias isn't a problem of concision, other than to say that perhaps you should exercise the ultimate concision on biased stories: Devote *no* words to them.

Don't step in to tell readers how they should respond to what you're about to tell them. Don't write in a nonfiction piece or a corporate report, for instance, that "The statistics will astonish you." Don't write in a short story that "The tale you're about to read will bring you to tears." In each of these cases, you're committing four errors:

• You're intruding. You're telling the readers, "Excuse me while I think for you," because you're really saying "*I think* the figures will astonish you." And, perhaps your intrusion borders on the insulting: "I must tell you the statistics will astound you because you're too stupid to realize it."
• You're using extra words.
• You're setting yourself up for a fall by raising reader expectations. In our case of the astonishing statistics, readers might respond, *OK. I'm expecting to be astonished, and anything less than astonishment will disappoint me.* Or, writing something like "What she said was hilarious" is about as tactful and adroit as saying, "Watch out, here

comes the punch line" when telling a joke. Just tell what she said. Let the readers react without your having set them up for a reaction. If they laugh, and think it's hilarious, you've accomplished as much as you could by introducing the hilarity. If they don't laugh, they're not disappointed because they weren't expecting to laugh in the first place. So, as the writer, you can march along gracefully or you can stumble clumsily and either way imply "I meant to do that." But if you telegraph (or state outright) your intentions, you set yourself up for someone watching—and realizing—your failure.

• You're not allowing your writing to do the work. Your writing hasn't surprised or delighted or astonished the reader; in other words, you have tried to provoke reaction, not evoke it. You're allowing the reader to watch that man behind the curtain at work.

Nor should you conclude by telling readers how they should react to what they've just read. The example of this that irritates me most is when the TV news shows us footage of a train crash that left seventeen people dead. The anchor looks at the camera and shakes her head. "Tragic story," she says. I guess we were too stupid to figure that out.

I've often seen such recapping on a less obnoxious scale in manuscripts over the years. For example, in a how-to manuscript, a writer gave a series of instructions, and then concluded, in a separate paragraph, "Simple, isn't it?" Well, it was simple, but pointing that out accomplished nothing. Confused readers weren't about to slap themselves on the forehead and say, "Gee, I guess you're right."

Give your audience credit. They can figure out how to interpret what you've written. Give your writing credit. It's strong enough to allow the readers to understand. I'm reminded of a 1982 TV show, *Police Squad*. ABC pulled it after four episodes because its humor was so zany, so dense, that the network couldn't possibly add a laugh track to it. "Without a laugh track," one network executive said, "the viewers won't know when to laugh." (*Police Squad* went on to become a cult favorite, and its producers expanded it into the quite popular, and laugh-trackless, *Naked Gun* movies.)

10. The Overkill
A certain type of bonsai groups four or five small trees in a single planter. These plants are not trees—they represent trees; this collection of figurative trees is not a forest—it represents a forest. This

is the opposite of the cliché about not seeing the forest for the trees, as we see no forest, but we know it is there, and we marvel at it. We see only one tenth of the iceberg that floats about looking for *Titanic*s to make itself famous with, but we know that the rest of it is there, and we respect it.

We needn't describe every leaf of the entire forest, every crevasse of the iceberg. In fact, sometimes all we need do is hint at the forest, suggest the iceberg. If we do more, we risk overkill, too many words and concepts, or words and concepts repeated too many times.

Areas in writing ripe for overdoing it include:

• Description. I once judged a play contest. One of the entries described the color of the characters' underwear.
• Pet phrases and verbal tics. I'll just have to get in line to decry "you know" in speech. In writing, tics are harder to spot. I tend to append "that sort of thing" to brief lists of items. That's unconscious. Conscious tics can present problems, too. Is Kurt Vonnegut's sprinkling his novels with "Hi ho" or "So it goes" writing device or writing tic? (I side with the former. Usually.)
• Argumentation. In most cases, you can state your point once and once only. Repeating your argument or your conclusions, if you have made them well the first time, not only is unnecessary, but also can drive the reader away. Readers don't want to feel they're being lectured, badgered or harangued. (And, as I'll discuss in a moment, sometimes making your argument *once* is too much, if you're convincing the already convinced.)
• Writing devices, such as onomotopaeia, analogies and alliteration. Describe the susurration of waves sliding along sand, and you have a gentle whisper of alliteration, sussing and hussing like the waves themselves. But splash on the sensual susurrating sound of the sea slipping sand aside, and you'll soon be able to listen to the sibilant hissing of the readers. They're sick of it.

Such problems erode your writing for these reasons:

Overkill is just wordy. (My making that point in a book on writing tight itself borders on overkill.)

Overkill is irritating. Has anyone ever touched you lightly on the shoulder two or three times? A dozen times? More? The first time, you hardly notice. But soon this light, undamaging touch, repeated without purpose, begins to drive you nuts. Continue to poke readers at the same place in your writing, and you'll end up with similar consequences. Take, for example, this overworked analogy that appeared in a magazine for writers some years back, in a report on writing for equine magazines: After a subhead reading "No gift horses here, but a corral full of dependables waiting to carry your brand," the author rides in with his lead: "You've got to have horse sense to write for horse magazines." After a snappy reference to how to keep your manuscript from returning to you "at a gallop," the author crosses the finish line with "you'll be ready to start a stable relationship with the horse magazines." That gets corny after about the second reference, embarrassing after the third. I should know; I wrote those examples in the way-back-when, and *I'm* embarrassed.

Overkill is boring. Have you ever come home from work, pulled the car into the driveway, turned off the ignition, opened the car door, got out of the car and walked to the front door, unlocked the door, taken off your coat, sat down in your easy chair, picked up a book, turned to page 1, and found an author given to describing every chronological detail about what is happening? That's what writer Jules Archer calls "expository diarrhea," and it afflicts fiction and nonfiction writers alike. Imagine your reader saying, "OK, I get the idea." That whole sequence could be reduced to "Have you ever come home from work and turned to page 1 of a book ... ?" The reader will make the mental leap required to fill in the action between coming home and picking up the book; the detail is overkill.

Overkill elevates a writing device or technique from background tool to front-and-center machination. Look at the example above about waves sliding along sand. There, alliteration establishes rhythm and the sound of the sea in the reader's mind—at an unconscious level, if the writing is working properly—because the very sound of the words echoes what the words are describing. It's a verbal sleight of hand. But extending the alliteration is like the magician saying, "Hey, the quarter didn't really disappear—I just palmed it." Be the good magician; never reveal your tricks.

And enthrall the reader with a range of tricks. In my tired equine analogies, I guess I was trying to be cute with my horsing around (you knew I was going to say it) with the language, but continual cuteness likely brought into question my writing ability. "OK, I've seen the rabbit come out of the hat a dozen times; you can't be a very good magician if you don't know any other tricks."

Overkill reduces credibility. Methinks thou dost protest too much. Translated, the cliché means "You spend so much time denying the charge, you must be guilty." Too much argumentation and too many words lead the audience *away from* the conclusion you'd like them to draw instead of toward it. Or, as the German proverb goes, "Loquacity and lying are cousins."

And if it doesn't sound like lying, it sounds like advertising (which sounds like a straight line to me). Take, for instance, an enticement such as "Stop by, and you'll get a free gift." Sometimes, I begrudgingly admit, saying "free gift," though redundant overkill, is necessary, as it's often used in direct mail, advertisements or other enticements aimed at people who distrust the message bearers. "Gift? There's *got* to be a string attached somewhere." Loosely translated, "free gift" means "Gift — trust us — we really mean what we say — gratis — no obligation." And you must admit that "free gift" is a lot shorter than all those pitiful assurances.

To combat overkill:

Think in threes, especially when giving examples, quoting sources, and so on. Three's hardly a crowd when it comes to writing. Three is perfect. Three's company, four's a crowd, two are untrustworthy (a stool with two legs falls over). And so much of our culture is based on the three. As examples:

Three strikes, and you're out.

The Trinity.

The Three Stooges (who are not the Trinity), not to mention the magical number of blind mice, little pigs, and bears who bedeviled Goldilocks.

We speak of Larry, Moe and Curly, even though Shemp made his appearances early on. We glorify Harpo, Chico and Groucho, but tend to forget Zeppo and Gummo. The lesson is that your writing act falls a little short if only Harpo and Chico are on stage. It will probably be blocked out of reader's minds if you trot out Zeppo after Groucho has taken his bows.

Even in this discussion, I relied on threes. Three examples of three (strikes, Trinity, Stooges), which were in turn appended by subsets of three (blind mice, little pigs, bears).

A fourth example is unneeded, for a couple of reasons. Pattern is established by the time of the third occurrence. Also—and importantly—threes satisfy readers on inner levels. The mystical three is indigenous to Western culture. For the Japanese, the number four has similar meaning—in fact, three is bad luck in Japan, which is one of the reasons Americans had trouble marketing golf balls over there.

Don't convince readers who are already convinced. A common problem with manuscripts I received while editing *Writer's Digest* was in the superfluous paragraphs talking people into becoming writers. The readers already were interested in becoming writers, or they likely wouldn't have bought the *Digest* in the first place. That was preaching to the faithful. This seems to crop up frequently. A magazine on home remodeling ideas recently included a paragraph about what percentage of home remodelers start in the bathroom—in an article on remodeling the bathroom. I contend that such statistics are unnecessary. The person reading the article is already interested in remodeling the bathroom, or wouldn't be reading the article. Besides, ultimately the reader is interested in only one part of that percentage—the part that he or she represents.

Don't modify the unmodifiable. If something has been destroyed, saying that it was "totally destroyed" is overkill. "Totally" is the 10 percent of "giving 110 percent." And an example of literal overkill: the phrase "kill 'em dead!" All this is related to "The Nonsensical," discussed on page 75 of this chapter.

In giving instruction or advice, make your point but once. Twice if the point is important. ("Remember, the electrical system must be off before you begin work or you risk great injury.") A third time—well, once is a suggestion, twice is a reminder, thrice is nagging. Rely on the permanence of print and the fact that readers can return to passages they didn't understand or consider important; that will help you resist repeating things.

Tread as lightly as possible. Aim for giving enough (information, background, whatever)—just enough. I discuss the subject of "the just enough" in more detail in chapter ten, on page 155.

11. The Inflated and the Deflated

"Word inflation" affects the language the same way financial inflation affects the economy. Individual coinages fall in value, have less power in the marketplace. We are a culture that of late tends to say "At this point in time" when "Now" will do.

There is, of course, sentence inflation, paragraph inflation and manuscript inflation. But these usually result from swallowing other elements of flab whole. Word inflation results from stretching the words themselves.

I once saw a sign in a printing plant lunchroom. "Carefulness counts." A nugget of good advice, yet a nugget that could be further mined. When you take care, you are careful—and when you convert the noun to the adverb, you add something, in this case, the syllable "-ful." When you convert the adverb back to the noun, you can take the "-ful" away (make it less "-ful"?), and return to "care." That is, unless you're an uncaring signmaker, who decides to pile on another syllable to make another noun, "carefulness," which means the same thing as the word at its core: "care." What's next at the signmaker? "Carefulnessosity?" Carefulness may count out in the printing plant. *Care* counts at the keyboard.

My own use of the word "concision" instead of the more prevalent and probably more accepted "conciseness" is a matter of form meeting function; "concision" is more concise, less inflated, than "conciseness."

To avoid word inflation:

✗ **Avoid the "Ness" monsters.** That's the term used by Richard Lederer, author of *The Miracle of Language*, in his Grammar Grappler column in *Writer's Digest*. "Carefulness" is one such monster, joined by "preciseness" (precision), "conciseness" (concision), "hungriness" (hunger), "pompousness" (pomposity), "indebtedness" (debt), and "zealousness" (zeal). Lederer adds "beautifulness" (beauty), "cruelness" (cruelty), "greediness" (greed), "proudness" (pride), and "thirstiness" (thirst).

But remember that "-ness" in itself isn't a monster. Such words as "viciousness," "promptness" and "vagueness" have no streamlined counterparts.

Avoid the syllable cysts. This is a matter of preventative medicine. Better yet, it's a matter of *preventive* medicine, since "preventative" contains a cyst, that extra "at" syllable. So it is with "combatative" instead of "combative."

Some of these result from sloppiness; some from confusion with the sounds of other words. Thus "telepathetic" (which should be used only to describe most TV shows) and "heart-rendering" (which sounds like part of the process of making cat food). Every so often, such confusion leads to some fascinatingly appropriate words, such as one I heard a while ago: "pall buriers."

Words afflicted with cysts are sometimes easy to spot, especially if the cysting leads to words that don't exist, such as "accompanyist" (accompanist), argumentative (a real word, but "argumentive" works as well), "capacitator" (capacitor), "exploitative" (exploitive), "irregardless" (regardless), "orientated" (oriented), "archetypical" (archetypal), "scrumptuous" — though longer in speech than in print — (scrumptious).

Some cysts mutate perfectly usable short words into perfectly usable long words, and are therefore more difficult to spot. For example: "I got a definitive answer." "Definitive" is a perfectly good word; depending on the context of the sentence, "definitive" might even be the right word — in the sense that the answer was the answer to end all answers. But if you meant only that you got a specific, conclusive answer, perhaps you meant to say, "I got a definite answer." And I've seen writers use such phrasings as "He's a *superlative* performer" — apparently when "super" isn't superlative enough.

In the following list of words, use the longer only when you really mean it; don't use it as a synonym for the shorter:

advancement/advance
argumentation/argument
depress/press
dosage/dose
eventuality/event
fallacious/false
formulating/forming
instantaneously/instantly
intention/intent
linkage/link
proffer/offer
protestation/protest

puzzlement/puzzle
simplistic/simple
sensationalistic/sensational
usage/use
utilization/use (or utility, as appropriate)

Then there's that odd class of cysted words that mean the same after you've added a supposedly negative prefix: loosen/unloosen, flammable/inflammable, ravel/unravel.

Don't be analytical about your writing; be analytic. Beware your "-ical" suffixes; perhaps "-ic" will do. "Mathematic" equations are just as precise as "mathematical" ones; sentences are more rhythmic without "rhythmical" in them. So it is with other words: dramatical, scientifical, geographical, fantastical, alphabetical, alphanumerical, historical.

But don't make such a trim every time you see the "-ical" ending; I once saw the word "mechanical" trimmed down to "mechanic," which is not the same. Also, I myself would likely use "analytical" before I would "analytic," simply because it is more commonly used, and is therefore more invisible.

Avoid the "oh gees," the "alities" and other ways to make words more wordish. A while back, when the coach of my hometown football team left his job after a losing season, a radio sportscaster told us, "The coach says he was fired; the team says he quit. Whatever phraseology you use, he's gone." Couldn't the sportscaster have said, "Whatever *phrase* you use"? After all, the principals involved were indeed using phrases, and not systems of setting words into longer units.

This seems to happen often, as if some writers and speakers take the attitude that they shouldn't use a word's root when they can use its rootology.

Avoid the problem: The methodology to this madnessology is to perform ologyectomy where appropriate, where the "root" word is the word you want. Do you want to say "terminology," or will "term" do? Do you want to say "biology," or will "bi" do? (As you see, as with all cutting, you can go to silly extremes.)

And if the "-ology" word is the right word, use it. Use it, I'm tempted to say, without a pology.

Similar constructions lead to similar problems. For example, how has "emotion" mutated into "emotionality"? "Potential" to "potentiality"? "Animal" (as in "animal drives") into "animalistic"? "Natural" into "naturalistic"? "Event" into "eventuality"? "Effect" the verb into "effectuate"? "Paralysis" into "paralyzation"? (I grant you that each version of the word has nuances, and, in some cases, completely different meanings. For instance, something that is "naturalistic" seems natural. The problem comes in when "naturalistic" is used when the context calls for "natural," which happens often.) I propose that to some writers and speakers, these larger words *feel* more like nouns or adjectives. Bulkier, they seem more solid. Nonsense. Words should be judged by their efficiency of communication, and not purchased by the pound.

Keep your "-ize" open. If you're forming a verb with an "-ize" suffix, first ascertain that the word you're converting doesn't already have a verb buried within. Consider the tortuous tale of the word "conceptualize." Let's back it up to the adjective "conceptual"; back "conceptual" to its base noun, "concept"; back *that* into the source verb "conceive." Why conceptualize ideas when you can more efficiently conceive them? The pity is that "conceptualize" mutates further into "conceptualization." Which is so much more a mouthful than "concept." (Keeping this word short seems awfully difficult — as evidenced by the related mutation, "conception.")

Describe what something is, not how it got that way. Some inflated words result from a tendency to describe not what something is but how it got that way: a husband and wife on the verge of divorce are not separate (what they are); they are separated (how they got that way). That seems to make sense, but only because "separated" is the familiar usage. But speaking of the "flattened plains of Nebraska" is using too much word for the job — the flattening took place a long time ago, so "flat plains" will do (and so will just plain "plains," which are rarely anything *but* flat). Similarly, "weak" is often an appropriate replacement for "weakened," unless you want to emphasize the process — the weakening — rather than the result — the weakness. Something that is "weakened" has changed; it used to be strong. Something that is "weak" has been that way for some time.

There are similar forces at work when writers use "complicated" as a synonym for "complex." In a loose sense, "complex" is what something is; "complicated" is how it got that way.

This principle applies to sentences as well. "I'm getting sick of all this advice." Getting sick? How about "I'm sick of all this advice"?

Examine clichés with critical eye. Good advice in general, but brought up here because inflated words can become enshrined in clichés. For instance, take the increasingly common phrase, "redoubled his efforts." A cliché because very little except efforts seems to get redoubled, and usually a redundancy because the user often really means "doubled" (which makes "redoubled" an encysted word), and more often really means "increased" (which makes "redoubled" simply the wrong word).

Beware the vogue word, the affected word. The "pretty" speech I discussed before can lead to word inflation. "The short word sounds, gee, pedestrian, so we'll pump it up a bit...." I like the versified example given by Joe Floren in his *Enough About Grammar*.

> *Clientele*
> Is hard to spele
> And, furthermore,
> it sounds like hele.
> *Clients* will work
> just as wele.
> (And sound less affected to boot.)

Inflating the Value of Inflation

Sometimes word inflation actually benefits the language: "aggression" and "aggressiveness" might be viewed as products of word inflation (though "aggression" actually preceded "aggress," the core of "aggressiveness"), but both are useful, representing distinct concepts. While both are nouns, "aggressiveness" (formed with as much grace as "carefulness") is a quality, while "aggression" is an action, an event. If word inflations lead to words with distinctive meanings and uses, fine. On the whole, though, it's best to not allow your words, your phrases, your manuscripts to balloon.

A similar analogy can be drawn between "word deflation" and financial deflation—both happen so rarely that when they do, more attention is paid to the deflation itself than to what it actually means to people. "To attrit," a coinage from the Persian Gulf War, actually makes great linguistic sense. It's a back formation, and it is within the scope of English language evolution. And how much simpler to say, "We will attrit the enemy," than to say, "We will reduce the enemy numbers through attrition." But, though shorter, "attrit" looks faddish, nouveau, even wrong. It is, therefore, distracting. (Odd that during the war, the word "aggression" never deflated to become the word "aggress." "*I aggress you*," he said, with foil in hand. There's a certain renaissance elegance to that. "*I aggressionize you*," it would be expressed today. Or, perhaps, "You are subject to my aggressionalizationnessosity.")

Avoid using the products of word deflation until they are commonly accepted. (Some products of word deflation will never be accepted. "Hopefully" is, unfortunately, one, even though it is both grammatically in line with several other commonly accepted constructions, such as "Frankly," and even though saying "Hopefully" is shorter and more direct than "I hope that" or "it is hoped that.")

A phrase deflation I'm coming to accept comes from the sports arena: "Defense" underwent some cross-training, going from noun to transitive verb. You now "defense" the pass rather than "defend against" the pass. The deflation is corrupted, however, when sports figures start to use "defense" as a synonym for "defend," as Cincinnati Reds shortstop Barry Larkin did when he said that he was using martial arts training to improve coordination, not to "defense himself."

That's one of the true tests of a new word created by either inflation or deflation. Does it perform a new function? If it merely supplants an older, perfectly acceptable word, the way Larkin used "defense," there's no good in it. If it, however, brings a new tool into the language, even if it's only subtly different, I applaud it. Take, for instance, "impact." There's great wailing over this noun's use as a transitive verb: "The reduction will impact you." No wailing from me. Though "impact" is often used as a synonym for the verb "affect," I argue that, used properly, the two words communicate different concepts.

"The reduction will affect you" means that, sure, some things will change, but we can talk about it and handling it shouldn't be any problem. "The reduction will impact you," with that forceful plosive in the middle of the word, means that, sit down, get ready, we have some talking to do. "Affect" is soft change. "Impact" is drastic, abrupt change, the way a moving car impacts a telephone pole.

Word deflation that has been accepted into the language includes such words as:

• The brief and informal "memo," much truer to itself than the lengthy and formal "memorandum."

• The brief (in a different sense) "bra," which I won't comment on further.

• The unencumbered "condo," which more clearly describes a less-obligated lifestyle than does the ponderous "condominium" (which sounds like it should appear on the periodic table of elements, anyway).

• "Auto" instead of "automobile," though the even shorter and more American "car" has pushed the more foreign "auto" aside, in kind of a linguistic refraction of real life.

• "Pants" are so much easier to slip on than those Victorian-sounding "pantaloons."

• "Flu" dumps out the inside of "influenza," much as it dumps out your insides.

• A "quote" is so much pithier than a "quotation," though the short form probably resulted from converting the verb instead of from word deflation.

Some word deflation as incorrect as the inflated "preventative" to watch out for includes: "accidently" instead of "accidentally"; "soley" instead of "solely"; "Smithsonian Institute" instead of "Smithsonian Institution"; "Jones' house" instead of "Jones's house"; "would of" instead of "would have"; "electric" instead of "electricity." (But beware: "subtly," not "subtlely," is correct).

12. The Invisible and Therefore Unnecessary

I have this odd mental block. My coffeepot at work is connected to a power strip; every night before I leave, I turn off first the pot itself, then the power strip. As I turn off the office lights, I check my desk lamp. It, too, is connected to the power strip, so if the lamp light is off, so is the power to the coffeepot. Invariably, by the time I get to the car, I'm thinking, "Did I turn off the coffeepot?"

My end-of-day coffeepot routine has become so familiar to me that it loses distinctness in my mind; it fails to make an impression.

Sure, I tell myself as I get into the car, I remember turning off the coffeepot. But am I remembering my doing that *today*, or yesterday, or one of the hundreds of other times I've performed the routine?

Much of our writing is populated with such coffeepot routines, so familiar to us and to our readers that they become indistinct, the opposite of memorable.

Certain understood words can drop out of our sentences because they are invisible. We know they're there, whether we see them or not. And even if they are there, we may not see them. How visible is the word "that" in "The book that I read last week"? It's so quiet a word that when we drop it out — "The book I read last week" — we don't miss it.

Spotting the Invisible

Certain *blocks* of words can perform similar disappearing acts — for example, clichés, and the cousins of clichés: inseparable adjective-noun combinations, standardized phrases and tired word pairs. Let's examine each:

The cliché. Clichés are like fast food hamburgers. No matter what city you eat them in, no matter what the language spoken in that city, the burgers taste the same. The clichés taste the same. They add the same nontaste to the annual report as they do to the best-selling novel. After a while, your taste buds become numbed.

Donna Levin in *Get That Novel Started!* explains her disdain for a uselessly invisible cliché, "sparkling eyes." She writes:

> I once heard a writer defend her use of that expression. "But Grandpa really did have sparkling eyes," she insisted, and then added, "I suppose I should have made that clear." Ah, yes, the sad thing is that clichés began as original, fresh phrases.... Trust me — readers will not stop to envision sparkling eyes anew, nor will they stop to tease out the nuances of the image of a young girl with "a spring in her step." Confronted with such familiar expressions, readers skip ahead to the next sentence while registering nothing except a vague sense of boredom.

Perhaps as big a sin as what is there — boredom — is what's *not* there — excitement. Using clichés robs you of opportunity to surprise readers. "Bitter cold" doesn't surprise. "Barren cold" does; "bitter heat" does.

The inseparable adjective-noun combination. Or, "Bitter Cold, Part II." This is a type of cliché, but common enough to warrant separate mention. Other examples include "raging inferno" (as opposed to the oft-described "unraging inferno"), and "doting parent." Does anyone other than parents, fans and admirers dote? I've never heard of a doting boss, a doting coach, a doting government administrator. (Which is, I suppose, a good thing.)

The standardized phrase. "You should never use standardized phrases," he chided gently. "Chided gently" is not only redundant ("chide" implies doing it gently), it's also so common that it seems that no one simply chides. Give me one good brusque chiding in a novel. Give me a rough-and-tumble chiding. Chide with extreme prejudice. Everyone who chides chides gently. Do not chide gently into that good night.

The tired word pair. I spoke of tautological pairs in the first section of this chapter, with such repetitive—and invisible—clichés as "aid and abet." No one, it seems, can abet a criminal without aiding them, too. The problem with those phrases is that they pair words that say essentially the same thing. Other pairs team words with different meanings, but are as clichéd and as invisible as the tautological pair. For instance:

> cats and dogs (raining *and* fighting)
> bent and broken
> breaking and entering
> fits and starts
> far and wide
> fast and furious
> high and dry
> if and when
> pure and simple
> sick and tired
> still and all
> tried and true
> wait and see

As I list these pairs, however, I can't help but think that they exist for a reason. Such buddy-buddy pairing of concepts can be considered linguistic teamwork implicit in the language or in how we use it. And we see it, as they say, day in, day out; year in, year out. (Which hauntingly reminds me of the phrase "garbage in, garbage out.")

The Advantage of the Invisible

Invisible is not all bad, however. There are times when you want the reader to glide over bland words, especially when the alternative is their bumping over words that are more visible than they should be—and are thus distracting.

The tools from your storytelling toolbox, in particular, should be quiet and invisible: Transitions, for instance. How much quieter to say, "Later, at home ..." than to spend four noisy paragraphs telling the reader how the person you're describing got home. Attribution— signaling who said what in quoted material and in dialogue—should similarly whisper.

That latter tool provides an especially good example of good invisibility. Four or five times a year during my stint at *Writer's Digest* I'd receive the manuscript titled with some variant of "76 Synonyms for the Word 'Said.'" At Writer's Digest Books, I received, with a straight-faced letter from the author's agent, an entire *book* of synonyms for the word "said."

I always said "No" to such manuscripts. I may have wanted to shout "No," to aver "No," to rage "No," to whisper "No," to scream "No," to pooh-pooh "No," to smile/growl/vocalize/spit/coo "No," but I just *said* "No."

In attribution, "said" is an invisible workhorse. Never worry about repeating "said" a number of times. If readers "can't see" it in the first place, how can they tire of it?

For that reason, and for the fact that the word *works*, "said" has few reasonable replacements. "And I mean it!" he raged. Rarely do you want to call that much attention to attribution, for four reasons:

1. "Saying" is shorter than "vocalizing" physically *and* mentally, because the latter is distracting; the former, invisible.

2. You've been forced to step in, to intrude.

3. If the reader must wait until the attribution to hear the rage in a character's voice, you've failed in demonstrating, through character action primarily, the character's anger. I would suspect that few rages are *not* accompanied by something physical you can describe to communicate rage. The coffee cup flung across the room. The blood-purpling of the face. The fist against the table. Describe those actions, and you don't have to lean on "he raged" to tell the readers what's going on. Flowery attribution is telling, not showing.

4. A function of attribution more important than communicating how something was said is communicating *who* said it. Attribution is a signpost.

Some synonyms have their place. For instance, "shouted" and "screamed" are often legitimate replacements:

> "I hate you!" he shouted.
> "I hate you!" he screamed.
> "I hate you!" he said.

Still, we're telling more than showing. Why not:

> His voice hurt my ears. "I hate you!"

Or, simply:

> "I hate you!"

"Asked" is a reasonable and usually invisible substitute when posing questions, but isn't always needed. You can say questions as well as you can ask them.

> "Are you leaving?" she questioned.
> "Are you leaving?" she asked.
> "Are you leaving?" she said.

The first sentence is loud and distracting. The second works quietly and efficiently. So does the third. Yet, there are differences, and context will dictate your choice. For example, in the third example, she is asking with a tad of resignation, in that "said" brings a flatness to the sentence that isn't in the middle version.

That's a lot of time spent in example for a couple of basic points:

Let important words speak loudly; let the unimportant hide in the shadows. And better yet, let important *concepts, actions, consequences* speak loudly. Let the words quietly lead to those concepts, actions, consequences.

The thinking applies as well to the "props" in your writing, the characters, settings and scenes that should speak quietly, as does the word "said," instead of extravagantly, as does the word "vocalized."

For example, in your short story, your characters go to a movie, and argue about who will pay for the tickets while a ticket-seller looks on. Does the seller look on impatiently? Tapping her toe? Sighing loudly and drumming her fingers? Probably, but does it matter what she does? Does it matter if she is a she? Do we have to describe even that much? For that matter, do we have to mention the ticket-seller at all? Perhaps. Readers will begin to wonder how other people react if the argument stretches on to any length. This is a public place, after all. These characters are in someone's way while the argument flares. After a while, the readers, being themselves polite sorts courteous of the people around them, will begin to feel uncomfortable—as uncomfortable, perhaps, as the people in line behind the arguing couple. So, a question, a very small question, is forming in readers' minds. The ticket-seller's looking irritated quickly and quietly answers that question, dispenses with it, and allows us to concentrate on what's important.

Or perhaps the ticket-seller advances the action: "The ticket-seller asked us to please make up our minds, and that made Harold all the angrier."

We've established the importance of the ticket-seller, then. But do we need to know how old she is, what she's wearing, what she had for lunch? No. Do we need to know how many people are standing behind our couple and what the eveningwear of choice seems to be? No. Giving that ticket-seller personality is like giving the word "said" personality. It stops *directing* readers' attention, and begins *commanding* it.

Like the bones of the skeleton within your own body, the building block elements that support your writing should remain unseen. If those bones become visible, you're hurting. So is your writing.

13. The Imprecise

The more specifically you express your thoughts, the less likely you'll turn to an empty, space-filling cliché or a jury-rigged series of words. "Swallowing quickly" is more than wordy; it's also imprecise. "Gulped" is quick and precise.

Imprecision is a particular sin in English, given the greater selection of words available to us. Writers in other languages might be forced into adverb-verb combinations we can sidestep with a single, more specific verb—we can say "leap" instead of "jump high." Stephen Baker is the ad man who gave us "Let your fingers do the walking through the Yellow Pages." A native Hungarian, he loves writing in English because of, among other features, its specificity. "For example, in my native Hungarian, jumpers could only *ugri* (jump). In America, they can *leap, hop, vault, spring, bound, bounce, caper, prance, buck, trip, bob, skip* or even *go hippity-hop*." English, he points out, has a larger vocabulary than any other language. "The larger the selection, the easier—and quicker—it is to get from one end of the sentence to the other. . . . For example, take the King James Bible, and put it next to its German version—same typesize, same format. The German translation is more than twenty-five pages thicker, or almost ten percent." This brings to mind Mikhail Gorbachev when he resigned the presidency of the U.S.S.R.: during his speech, broadcast live, his mouth seemed to form far more words than were used by his English translator, who spoke leisurely.

Specificity is honed clarity; it eliminates any descriptions and modifications and elaborations you might otherwise need to communicate exactly what you mean. Specificity not only shortens your writing, but also reduces mental length by answering readers' questions immediately. For example:

Vague: In a city somewhere in the East . . .
Better: In Charleston, West Virginia . . .

Vague: I left shortly after 6:00.
Better: I left at 6:03.

Vague: I ordered one of those fancy umbrella drinks with Triple Sec and orange juice.
Better, maybe: I ordered a hurricane.

Note, however, that in the last example, specificity might work against you. If your audience doesn't know what the heck a hurricane is, you might have to explain it: "I ordered a hurricane—one of those fancy umbrella drinks with Triple Sec and orange juice."

Now, note how even a sentence made *longer* by specificity picks up speed:

Vague: I took my keys from a hook near the refrigerator and walked to the car.
Longer and better: I snapped up my keys, hanging from a hook near the rusted Fridgidaire, and strode straight to the Mustang.

This is longer but swifter because it answers questions immediately: What kind of car? How did he walk? Just what might be going on? Specificity locks clear images into the readers' minds, allowing them to picture and to watch rather than to wonder and more passively observe.

To work toward specificity, ask questions of your copy: How? Why? In what way? Can you be more specific?

Let's apply such questioning to some vague description, for example: "John is a pleasant person." *In what way?* Well, he smiles a lot, and always say hello. Let's just say *that*, then: John smiles often, and always greets you politely. That's longer, but more mentally efficient in its specificity.

Then let's apply the questions to something longer — the following imprecise sentence, for instance: "My goal is to gain the presidency." *How?* How do you gain the presidency? You run for election. "I am running for the presidency" is more direct than the first version.

Specificity is often your tool for eliminating weak verbs, such as "gain." For example, "I handled the staff training." The weak verb there is "handled." How did you handle it? Change the sentence to "I trained the staff" if that's how you handled it, or "I supervised the staff training" if *that's* how you handled it.

14. The Clever and the Show-offy

As an editor, I was once quite fascinated by the cute subhead. At one point, I was editing a story about a photographer in China, working with a tour guide from an outfit named Lotus Tours. I edited in a subhead, "The Lotus, My Shepherd," and was darned proud of it. I'm not proud of it anymore. Fine pun, with three problems:

• It was too clever. The reader had to think about it. That time spent thinking about it hurt the article as much as any deadwood words or paragraphs that similarly slowed down the reader.

• It was out of character with the rest of the piece. Had the article been a pun-filled romp rather than a fairly straightforward account of freelance photography in China, it might have worked. As it was, the pun was jarring, and obstructive.

• It did nothing to help the reader through the article. It was cute and nothing more. If I'd wanted only cute, I could have published a little picture of a kitten in the space and accomplished just as much.

With subheads as with everything else in your prose, eliminate the distracting kittens and retain the invisible workhorses.

Long after the Soviet Union broke up, officially dismantling Russian Communism in the process, a writer referred to the "communauts, I mean cosmonauts" then still at work in a space station. Let's not let political reality get in the way of a clever line, shall we? Even if Russian Communism had been alive, the pun would still have gotten in the way of a straightforward story of an extension of a space station tour of duty. "Commu-nauts" is also self-conscious author intrusion, tinged with commentary, and painted with the author's assumptions. How do we know they were Communists? Not all Soviets were members of the Party. Worst of all, it was a stretch for a pun. If you have to explain a play on words, you're wasting space and time not only on the play but also on the explanation.

Avoid showing off, whether it is the active allure of arresting alliteration, the pow-pow-pow of onomotopoeia, the sublime internal rhyme, casting puns upun the reader, or being cute or offbeat in leads, in transitions or in conclusions. These offenses add primarily to mental length, but add to the physical, as well, as you scramble to draw together words that fit into your verbal concoction. To make a weak pun about "commu-nauts" fit his story, the writer had to step back and expend words explaining what he was up to. Another example: Effective alliteration often works best when only a couple of words are involved. Expanding much beyond that, into the show-offy string of four or five alliterative words (as discussed in the section on "overkill"), and you're using not just too many distracting words, but too many words, period.

Avoid these elements altogether? No. Used effectively—and here I mean subtly—these elements add power and grace to your writing.

Used ineffectively—blatantly and self-consciously—they add circus-poster hype to it.

15. The Nonsensical

I once saw a sign posted outside a house: "Free Kittens for Sale."

That the sign was longer than it had to be was the least of its problems. I got the message, I guess. But I didn't buy/take any kittens. I *did* remember the sign. The length of the sign is not in the number of letters or words in it, or in how long it took me to read it, but in how long it stuck in my mind, and in how long I puzzled over it. "Free" and "for sale" are opposite terms; the sign was nonsensical.

Nonsense is another one of those mental lengtheners, and with a quick nip and tuck on the nonsensical, we reduce length both physical and mental. Nonsense can take the form of the oxymoron, as in the kittens example. It can take the form of the impossible, as with "a little pregnant." Or it can take the form of the illogical, as in the standard pair "if and when." For example, "If and when your loan goes through, we'll conclude the deal." In that sentence, "when your loan goes through" says that it *will*; there's no "if" about it.

16. The Beautiful

Ever had a crush? In the eighth grade, I had two. One was my algebra teacher, who I loved from that adolescent afar for what seemed like adolescent eternity, though it probably lasted longer—say, four or five weeks. My other love was a shapely thing, with plenty of elegance and style. This one was a word: "catafalque," an ornamental scaffolding used to support a body lying in state. Oh how I struggled to fit that word into my fiction, but it never worked. "The space station exploded, a funeral pyre on a celestial catafalque"—or some such embarrassing phrasing in an equally embarrassing science fiction novel.

As I did my eighth-grade algebra teacher, I romanced "catafalque" at a distance. I still love that word, even though I just now looked it up to make sure I remembered its meaning correctly.

"Abyss" was a similar love affair, to this day unfulfilled.

Let's face it. We're word people, drawn to the beauty and grace of language and its components. And like starry-eyed lovers, we want our gorgeous consorts at our sides. That's OK, but let's try not to be Woody Allen, putting our current loves into each movie we make. *Sleeper* would have been a better movie without Diane Keaton, and almost any manuscript I write will be better without "catafalque." Except for that science fiction novel. Nothing by its inclusion or its absence would have improved it.

3. Prewriting Tight

*Y*ou're familiar with those pre-wash laundry products: the soaks and stain sticks that attack dirt and stains before you pop the clothes into the wash.

I contend, though, that the best pre-wash is pre-vent. Don't stain the clothes in the first place.

So it is with writing tight. Don't stain the prose in the first place.

Editing your writing for concision is so much easier if you keep the wordiness to a minimum even at the first-draft stage. That in mind, here's how to make sure the writing goes down onto the page tight:

Don't worry about prewriting tight. We've all heard that the best way to trip a centipede is to ask it which leg it moves first (assuming the centipede speaks English, I suppose). Don't be a centipede at the keyboard; don't worry about the tiny missteps at the expense of the manuscript as a whole. I've found that if I'm self-conscious about my writing, the sentences and words I put on the page are longer than they would be had I simply gotten to work putting down *ideas* instead of *words*. I concoct phrasings that are deliberate, considered and studied. Now, deliberate, considered and studied are good in legal briefs. *Flow* isn't much of a concern in such documents.

You have too much to worry about at the keyboard as it is. Are the ideas good enough? Am I presenting the ideas in their most effective order? How can I make all this stuff *credible*, for heaven's sake? Big challenges. Don't make them all the more difficult by worrying about the fact that you happened to let "at this point in time" slip by you. You'll get it later. Consciously tell yourself that: You'll get it later. Later that writing session, as a matter of fact: At the end of every writing session, review what you've just written.

Feel free to edit at this point; in fact, by reminding yourself as you start that you'll spend time picking nits at the end of the writing, you'll free yourself from fussing over the nits—and possibly freezing up—during the writing.

The benefits of such postwriting review loop around to reducing your self-consciousness at the beginning of the next writing session. As you review what you've written, dig out what you did right, not only what you did wrong. In fact, the postwriting review I describe can instead be handled as a prewriting review at the next writing session. (Or why not at both times?) Kit Reed in her *Revision* even suggests starting each writing session by retyping a couple of pages from the previous session. "This gives you continuity. The pages you retype will get better in the process and you'll have a running head start on the new day's work."

It gives you confidence as well as continuity. As I point out elsewhere in this book, noting the good writing—taking justifiable pride in what you're doing—gives you all the more energy and confidence when you sit down to face tomorrow's blank page.

And make it *tomorrow's* blank page. To reduce the potential for self-conscious writing, take some old and savvy advice: Write every day. If that centipede walked only on alternating Saturdays, it would have to give some thought to which leg *does* go first.

Still, take a few lessons in prewriting tight as you do all the lessons of this book, store them in the subconscious—forget about them on the conscious level—and get to work.

Outline by memory. Review your notes carefully, then put them aside. On a separate sheet of paper, jot down the key points you want your nonfiction piece to make, the primary instructions your memo should communicate, the crucial scenes that should occur in your novel. Organize them into a logical flow.

This won't be the outline you use; as you later compare it with your notes or with preliminary outlines, you'll see that you left out significant topics and items. You'll also see that you left out *insignificant* topics and items. Chop them out.

The memory outline has employed your mind's natural tendency to assign priorities. It remembers the important, while it pushes the unimportant aside. If you forgot it while preparing your quick outline, consider forgetting it entirely.

This is, in a sense, an extension of point #1—forget about things on the conscious level and get to work. The subconscious has much to offer you.

The outline-by-memory theory, of course, has its flaws, especially when applied to *my* memory. Why is it I can't remember my wife's birthday but can detail the first five picks of my fantasy baseball team from seven years ago? (In the outline of my life, something is out of balance here.) Just because you remembered it while outlining by memory doesn't mean it's important. You also tend to remember the interesting, the unusual and the out-of-place.

Yet, I'm reminded of the writer who never wrote down ideas. "If it's a good one, I won't forget it," he said.

Write; don't just weave facts and quotes and — especially — your notes. Don't transfer your notes directly from notepad to manuscript. Don't feel obliged to uproot entire quotes from interview transcripts. Use them as source material, not as the actual material.

Granted, some people take very complete notes, especially when they flesh out handwritten notes at the keyboard (which, by the way, is a good idea, especially after an interview; review your notes and fill in things you remember but didn't have time to write down). There are times when my jottings start out telegraphic, but as I warm to my subject, the squiggled abbreviations stretch into full sentences that often appear intact in the final manuscript. Within this book are numerous occurrences of notes that became final text (this paragraph is not one of them).

But doing so increases your chances of letting wordiness slip by. You jot notes about the office of an interview subject. "Ficus tree standing in one corner," you scribble into the notebook. "There's a ficus tree standing in one corner," you type later, when perhaps you should type "A ficus stands in one corner."

As dangerous is when your interview subject says "There's a ficus tree standing in one corner," or something similar, and you quote her word for word. Though I believe in the sanctity of the quote, I don't believe that sanctity and verbatim transcription are the same thing. If you trimmed the quote to "A ficus stands in one corner," you are not misquoting her — unless the more concise version communicates something false about the subject: It makes her sound more formal, more educated, whatever, than she actually is. You can clean up grammar in quotes. You can help the subject get to the point more quickly between those quotation marks. As long as you don't misrepresent the person or what the person is saying.

There's a fiction corollary to this, in that sometimes writers throw in "umms" and such to replicate speech. "That's how people talk," these writers argue. Granted. But not a valid argument. When writing dialogue, you're not trying to put to paper what people *say*, but what other people *hear* those people say. Readers are "hearing" with their eyes as they read your manuscript.

In real life, when we listen to someone speaking, what we hear and what we register are two different things. Someone can pop into my office and say, "Oh, hi, you're here. I didn't—um—you said that—anyway, umm, I need to know where to put that, uh . . . " and then he points at my in-basket to indicate a report we'd discussed a few minutes before. I *hear* all that in the very physical sense. But what my brain *registers* is "Hi, you're here. I didn't think you would be, because you said you'd be gone. Anyway, I need to know where to file that report." Listening, I have filled in blanks and screened out "static." I should do the same while writing, because I want to put to paper what I the writer want you the reader to perceive about the conversation. If I want you to perceive that we discussed a report, I would put to paper the latter "transcription." If I wanted you to perceive something else, I would transcribe it differently. If I wanted you to think that the person was indecisive and a bit scattered, I'd keep the quote intact.

Writing is a matter of selective communication—and we the writers are doing the selecting. The reader believes that, as we selectively communicate, we pass on only what we believe is important, so what we pass on takes on perceived importance. If we insert an "umm," the reader infers that we must have done so for a reason. In this instance, let's prove the reader right, and include only material that has a strong reason for being there.

"Writing-by-compilation" is a particular danger if you work at the word processor, because of its ability to capture and manipulate keystrokes. Word processing allows you to "grow" writing within text files, using a technique that has been dubbed "the organic page." Here's how it works:

You start writing, say, a novel. You have a general plot idea, and some characters come to mind. You open a text file, and type in a few character descriptions, two or three snatches of dialogue, maybe a bit of action. Then, as you work out the plot, you begin to type in a general outline. Part one will take place five years ago. Part two will take place three years ago. Part three, which wraps up the book, takes place in the present. Then individual chapters start to come to mind. So you go to part one, hit the return a few times, then type in what will happen in individual chapters. Chapter three, you see, is a good place to introduce your villain, so you move his description from where you had typed it elsewhere in the file, and under the notes for chapter three. Then there was that bit of dialogue you thought the villain would engage in to introduce him to the reader — you move the dialogue into the notes for chapter three, as well.

And on it goes. You insert notes into the appropriate places. Some of the notes are more complete than others — you can possibly touch them up and let them stay in the book. More notes, more ideas, and you begin writing. Then you strip away some of the other notes, and eventually, a novel begins to take shape. You split the chapters off into separate files, and continue growing and writing the book within each file.

That's a useful, time-saving process. You don't have to retype notes that need no further polish, that will stand without change. You can move text around to see how it links with other parts of the book. You can imbed notes to yourself in the text, saying that you should check this fact or elaborate on that point.

And you can go completely haywire in overwriting.

Say that in your notetaking you wrote a quick but insightful description of your protagonist as you sketched out an action scene. At a later writing session, while piecing together some of the protagonist's background, you describe him again. Still later, you contrast the physical description of the protagonist against that of another central character.

Each set of notes and what they cover — the action scene, the character background, the description of the other character — have their place in the novel, and you move each from the notes file to appropriate chapters.

And you end up with three independent descriptions of your character, two of them unneeded.

In your nonfiction piece notetaking, you think of a perfect analogy to express your central point. Then you think of an anecdote that supports it. That leads to another incisive analogy. And by picking up all that text with the block-move feature in the word processor, three bits of copy accomplishing the same thing are plopped into different parts of your manuscript.

Or for your profile, you transcribe the interview directly into a word-processing file. You type in exactly what your profile subject said, even though he took some time in making an important point or two. Later, with cursor and block-move function, you lift out some of the interview, place quote marks around it, and slip it into the appropriate part of the story, even though the quote is littered with redundancy.

And you may never notice those problems. The ability to capture your keystrokes so that you don't have to retype passages is all well and good, but because you are "gluing" things together rather than rehandling them, you lose the opportunity to reconsider and possibly revise these blocks of text. Redundancies can slip by (not to mention the danger of forcing transitions between blocks of text, when a front-to-back retype would give you greater sense of how the article is flowing, and greater opportunity to create the needed flow).

In such cases, the organic page becomes the cancerous page. Verbal growth out of control.

That's why it's important to employ the word processor in your head. You should process information and words to the page. Don't just transcribe them. Don't just transfer them.

Beware the wordiness potential of your writing rhythms. Are you a slow starter? Peck at the keyboard until you get back into the rhythm of thoughts flowing into words.

Many writing instructors warn you of the wordy or unnecessary lead. Look to the second or third paragraph of your story, they say. Your lead might be there, because many writers take a while to "warm up," or to "clear their throats." Wordy and unnecessary leads can also result from indecision about your starting point—in which case, you're warming up not to the writing but to the subject.

Agreed—but the advice doesn't go far enough. It assumes that you warm up only once per manuscript—when writing your lead. Fact is, you warm up maybe dozens, sometimes scores of times per manuscript: every time you sit down to work on it. And in all but one case, you're warming up in the middle of the manuscript. Look to the lead for throat-clearing material. Then look beyond the lead, as well.

If you know you're a throat-clearer, battle the resulting wordiness in two ways.

• Clear your throat at the typewriter with a project not intended for publication: a letter to a friend, poetry you're writing for fun, a verbatim retyping of some Hemingway to get not only fingers but also brain cells in motion.

• Place a symbol in the manuscript that signals "I started my writing day here" when you revise it, a # or a ˆ — or if you have a word processor, a ‡ or a § or whatever else ASCII text can give you. When editing the article, search for that symbol, manually or electronically, and examine carefully the material that follows.

Similarly, become aware of your rhythms as you write. Don't be self-conscious about it, or we're back to our centipede problem. But learn the "feel" of the writing as you put it to the page. If you struggle to include a sentence, a fact or a point, all the while saying to yourself, "I gotta find a way to get that in," maybe you don't gotta. If the fact isn't slipping into the flow of your writing, yet you're not facing similar problems getting the rest of the material down, maybe it just plain doesn't belong there. It doesn't matter if it's pertinent, useful, interesting, whatever — if it doesn't slip into the paragraph naturally, it probably isn't crucial. By *not* getting those facts or whatever that you "gotta find a way to get in," you can save space, and possibly spare yourself verbal gymnastics.

Don't misinterpret your rhythms, though. The writing that comes slow and awkward one day might result from your simply having trouble getting the words down, not from your getting the wrong ones down. I'm speaking more of those times of relative struggle, when the writing is going well, except for that one little section. . . . Maybe that one little section is telling you something.

Related to the problems of writing rhythms, beware the repeated word. Minor point, but something to watch for. Repeated words can pop up in your manuscript when you stop in the middle of a sentence and then . . . then after some thought, you start writing again. It's a common unconscious error to retype the last word on the page or the screen when you pick up the writing, as if you're pouring the word back in to prime your writing pump.

No writing is ever going to get onto the page stain-free, however. So, after prewriting tight, it's time to do some postwriting tight.
It's time to start editing.

4. Testing Your Writing for Flab

*I*n our house, there's no such thing as a quiet evening watching television. I take my self-imposed role as language cop too seriously, and find myself yelling "freeze!" at the criminals who so frequently perpetrate the language crimes TV seems so intent on promoting. Literally yelling. Usually at newstime.

"The seventeen-year-old teen . . ." the news anchor says, and I snap out, "As opposed to the seventeen-year-old crone." Of course, I don't hear anything else about the teen, because I'm stepping in, carping about the deadwood words that are being thrown at me, not listening.

I try to snap at my manuscripts as often as I do the TV, try to make the same critical-slash-cynical demands of my words that I do those of the news blow-dries. If I don't, the readers won't listen to me, either.

It's a good test I'm giving to the news anchor, one of several tests we can apply to our prose, lest we fail as writers and have to take menial jobs like reading newscopy.

To identify and eliminate wordiness, use the following exercises to constructively "yell" at your writing. The first nine test your manuscript at draft stage. The tenth tests your writing *after* you have sold it and offers clues to improving your writing in general.

Apply the "as opposed to" test. Question your writing (especially your phrases) the way I questioned the TV newscaster — using "as opposed to?"

You write, "green in color." *As opposed to what? Green in height?* "I ran quickly." *As opposed to running slowly? Only if you're a clock.* It's OK to be a bit smart-alecky about the process. If you're not, your editor will be.

You write, as one newswriter did, "The stock market closed early Christmas Eve because of the Christmas holiday." *As opposed to closing early because of that rampant hemorrhoid epidemic?* Granted, there may have been other reasons for the closing, but leaving off the phrase "because of the Christmas holiday" probably wouldn't have too many readers saying "how come?"

Apply this to every level of the writing, from the potentially tautological phrase like "drop down" (as opposed to dropping up?) to the long paragraph explaining that researchers are scrambling to find a cure for cancer because it kills so many people each year (as opposed to finding a cure so you have a great opening line in singles bars?). Now, if there's an unusual reason researchers are scrambling for a cure — to develop a series of profitable drugs for a pharmaceutical company, for instance — explain why.

Apply the "so what?" test. At my publishing company, we generate "trip reports" that describe our business travel and its results. And because we *are* a publishing company, we wax a bit eloquent in our trip reports. "The office of House of Agents is in a beautiful New York brownstone, its woodwork rich and well preserved, with a fine glazed-tile fireplace in each agent's office." *So what, Brohaugh? Did you sign the contract or didn't you?* If you can't answer "so what?", you can usually delete it. *Usually*, because some material that fails this test can still be crucial to your manuscript — if you can project that the *reader* can answer so what: "So, I want to know."

You can't answer "so what?" in your head. You must answer it in the manuscript. "So what if there's a gun on the wall in the first scene?" Show so what. Someone must fire the gun in the final scene. "So what if the agent has a fabulously expensive office?" Explain so what. Point out that his expenses and plush surroundings may explain why his contract demands were so unreasonable; he must pay for them somehow. Besides, his opulent surroundings demonstrate that he's used to getting contract concessions from the editors he works with.

Another way to ask "So what?" is "Who cares?", which leads us directly into our next test.

Ask yourself, Will the reader miss this word/sentence/paragraph/chapter? This takes the "so what?" test a needed step further. Some material can pass the "so what?" test, yet can and should be eliminated anyway. OK, I can prove why I describe fancy fireplaces in my trip report, but will my readers miss the information if I take it out? Will the report of what I've accomplished be less understandable, or make it *seem* less complete?

Will the reader, for instance, look at your article on Corvettes and say, "Hey, why aren't there a few pages on the history of the steering wheel in this article?" Take those pages out.

In an article about editor-writer relationships I wrote for the *Novelists, Ink* newsletter, I wrote: "Give me the benefit of the doubt that if, for instance, I don't respond to a request or a submission immediately, it may be that a number of requests or submissions were first in line. Or if I respond a little more curtly in a letter than perhaps you'd like, it's because my writing eight curt letters during a day accomplishes more than five chatty ones." My editor judiciously deleted the second sentence. It answers "So what?" properly, as it addresses a specific situation, and it relates directly to the point that work schedules often dictate the level and extent of the editor-writer relationship. That's so what. But will the reader miss it? No.

The "miss it?" test can be applied even on the smallest levels. For example, obituaries might most commonly appear in the daily newspaper, but they can appear in weeklies (*Time* magazine, for instance). So "daily obituaries" is not strictly a tautology. Yet, it boils down to the fact that the reader doesn't care about the difference between "I read the daily obituaries" and "I read the obituaries," so why use the extra word?

As I hinted, material can fail the "so what?" test and yet be essential to your manuscript if it passes the "Will the reader miss this?" test. Readers can miss seemingly nonessential information. Descriptions of the weather, for instance, might have little impact on the plot of your mystery—but are you failing to satisfy the reader's craving for mood and atmosphere if you leave them out? Readers' expecting certain information, whether or not it's crucial, is enough to satisfy the "so what?" test. *So what if it's raining continuously through the first three chapters of this mystery?* In and of itself, perhaps, so nothing. But if my mystery had nothing to signal mood, you'd miss it.

If material answers reader questions or fulfills reader expectations but performs no other function, it is not superfluous.

Test your manuscript for repetition. If you're writing nonfiction, go through your final manuscript and jot a key word or phrase that describes the purpose of each paragraph. The shorter the phrase the better—short keeps you from defining the purpose too broadly. Then review the key words you've jotted in; if you discover two or more that are similar, compare them. You may find that you're making the same point in two different places. (You may also find that you've scattered related but necessary material; you might want to draw the sections closer to one another to improve the manuscript's flow.)

Better yet, go through your notes *before* writing the article. Identify potential repetition before it moves onto the page.

You might similarly annotate an outline, prepared before or after the writing, with such key words.

You can do the same with fiction. One of your key phrases might read, "Establish Scrooge as penurious," and you might end up jotting it a few times through your manuscript. Cut the superfluous attempts at characterizing Scrooge? If they are indeed superfluous. But one paragraph demonstrating Scrooge's primary characteristic might not be enough; more might be needed to demonstrate the depth of the penuriousness, and the fact that Scrooge displays *retractable* penuriousness.

Weigh your writing against its purposes. On page 12, I suggest that you define the primary and secondary purposes of your manuscript, then weigh the manuscript itself against those purposes. I won't repeat them here, except to extend the concept to smaller scales within the manuscript: the theme of a paragraph.

Writer Gary Provost once noted in *Writer's Digest* that to retain focus within paragraphs, writers should test material in each graph against the paragraph's topic sentence. First, establish the topic sentence, the one that states the central theme or purpose of the paragraph. The topic sentence needn't appear in the writing itself; the topic sentence of *this* paragraph is "Here's how to identify a topic sentence."

Then, test other sentences to make sure they support the topic sentence. Provost writes:

Here's an example.

"Facing them were over 600 passengers of the liner and enough cameras to start a movie studio. Obviously, this was a special wedding. In fact, all America will be invited, as it was filmed for *Real People*, the series Purcell has co-hosted for the last five years. Five years is a kind of magic figure to television producers, because after five years a show is considered an appropriate candidate for syndication. The wedding segment will air this Wednesday, Nov. 2."

The topic sentence in that paragraph is "Obviously, this was a special wedding." The sentence about 600 passengers on a luxury liner, filming the wedding for television and broadcasting the wedding all support the idea of it being special. They pass the test. The sentence that does not pass the test is the one about syndication. That has nothing to do with the wedding being special. Get rid of it.

Weigh the balance of the manuscript. I recommend that you outline your manuscripts—fiction, nonfiction (don't outline the haiku)—either before you write it, or after. Or both, if the manuscript has changed in the writing. Prewriting outlines help direct your composition; postwriting outlines help you evaluate it. An outline can help you gauge the balance of coverage in your manuscript. The outline, by its nature, clearly shows you which subjects are of secondary and tertiary interest.

If you don't write your manuscript to a traditional outline, sketch out an after-the-fact outline of the piece when it's complete. Map it out briefly. If you outlined the piece before or as you wrote it, amend the outline to reflect the final shape of the manuscript.

On the outline, note how many lines each outline item occupies in the manuscript itself: how long is each of the A sections of the outline? how long the B sections within the A sections? how long the C sections? Ideally, all the A's should be about the same length—so, too, the B's and C's, compared not to all B's and C's, but to the B's and C's within the same A section. If one of your B's is twice as long as another within the same section, perhaps the longer one is too wordy, or too detailed. And if that B is longer than an entire A section, you have a real balance problem.

Now, achieving balance can mean a shorter manuscript—if you balance by reducing the size of relatively unimportant material. It can also mean a longer manuscript if you balance by spending more time on the important material. That's OK, unless doing so threatens a word count you must adhere to.

Also, achieving balance doesn't necessitate automatically cutting long passages of secondary material. Examine the role of that material in the manuscript. Maybe the length isn't wrong. Maybe your classification of that long material as secondary is wrong. That's why amending your outline is important. One amendment might be elevating something you thought would turn out to be minor to its proper status.

The outline is going to serve you most often in nonfiction; in fiction, outlines serve you as tools for plotting and storytelling chronology, not as tools for weighing balance. So look for balance these ways:

• *Character balance.* List your characters on a page. Next to each name, tally the number of pages the character appears on. If spear-carriers (an old stage term for extras) appear more often than banner-carriers, something's wrong. Don't allow the spear-carriers to steal the show by giving them too much personality and coverage in relation to the main characters. Don't allow them to dominate the book with their physical presence. Trim them back (or give them more significant roles; if they interest you that much, perhaps you should give them a promotion).

• *Plot balance.* Identify your primary plot and its various subplots. Roughly calculate how many pages you devoted to the primary plot, and how many to the subplots. If the number of pages devoted to subplots is equal to or greater than that devoted to the main plot, you're spending too much time on the secondary material (or too little on the primary). The outline will be of some help here; compare your findings against the outline. Have you spent half of your manuscript laying a plot thread that takes 10 percent of your outline? Perhaps you've gone overboard. (Perhaps, too, you've naturally gravitated toward a more interesting story. Outlines are made to be revised and, often, ignored. Let the strength of the story and not the strength of the outline dictate the tale you tell.)

• *On a looser level, the balance of other fictional elements: including balance of characterization, description and plotting.* I've been speaking about the balance of elements within plot, within characterization. Now we speak of the balance of these elements against the other elements—the balance of plot versus, say, description. All description and no plot makes Jack a dull storyteller. I recall estimates that a story should devote about a third of its wordage to characterization so readers know who's involved, a third to plot so they know what's happening, and a third to description so they know how and where the story is taking place. I will offer no such guidelines, as genres differ, stories differ, story*tellers* differ. As one quick example, "literary" fiction seems to call for an imbalance favoring characterization over plot, at least in the stereotyped "definition" of literary fiction. Let's leave the advice at this: Be sensitive to any of these elements dominating your story—unless the story demands it.

I've heard of writers who color code manuscripts to help them visualize the balance of various elements. With a highlighting pen on a copy of the manuscript, they mark, for instance, dialogue in blue, description in yellow, action in pink, introspection and internal monologue in green. Paging through, they can get a feel for what's dominating, then decide if the dominant elements should be trimmed back. A lot of pink in an action-adventure novel is fine, but if blue is taking over, perhaps dialogue should be slimmed down.

Check nonfiction for such balances, as well. Check the balance of quotes, anecdotes, transitions, summaries, statistics, and so on. Some elements will naturally dominate. You must determine if they dominate because they should, or because you've simply been too loquacious in those areas.

There are no formulas for balance, no hard 60:40 ratios to adhere to. In fact, applying numbers to your writing this way is dangerous. I doubt that you'll analyze your writing with this system more than once or twice if you do indeed try it. The analysis will reveal any propensity to overemphasize secondary material or to repeat primary material; it won't give you vector factors or curve ratios that will streamline your writing the way engineers can streamline car designs using a wind tunnel. Test a few manuscripts with these numeric and color-coding balance exercises, and you'll eventually be able to sense imbalance as you read and review your copy.

Test your manuscript for overextension. One thing leads to another—as you discuss your primary topic, you branch off briefly to discuss related supporting topics. From the supporting topics, you branch off briefly to discuss topics that support *them*. Keep branching, and you stray away from your central topic; you're overextending into the superfluous.

To test for overextension, lay out your manuscript with a bubble diagram. In the center is the core of your manuscript (whether article, poem, report, or, in the case of the following example, the first chapter of a book about writing tight)—this is your main focus, your "stem" in keeping with the organic analogy. Draw it like this:

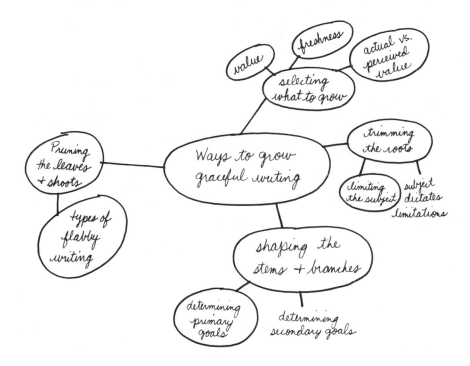

As a general guideline, you must branch off once from the main subjects to elaborate, you almost certainly will branch off again from the elaboration, but you should be wary of branching off again from *that* subsubject.

You could argue that the length of your manuscript dictates the number of levels you can slip away from your primary topics. A long multigenerational novel, for instance, can be quite complex, with scores of characters and multiple plot lines. But even here, I contend that we are dealing not with a heavily branched system, but one with a very long single stem, with many closely linked stem branches. (And multiple plots? Here we have more than one stem, *intertwined* and closely related in theme or mood.)

We could entangle ourselves in this ivied branch system metaphor all day, so allow me one more comparison: The farther away the shoot from the stem, the larger the plant, and the smaller the percentage of the shoot's contribution to the overall health of the plant. Branches—and words and sentences and ideas—should feed directly into the core of whatever it is we're growing at all times.

Read your manuscript as a reader. Simplistic advice, but appropriate. Read your memo, short story, play, whatever, as if you'd never seen it before. (Putting it aside for a time after you've written will help.) I know you can't completely suppress your knowledge of the manuscript, and that's fine; in fact, it's part of the process, as I'll explain in a moment.

As you read, don't question words or phrasings (yet, don't miss the opportunity to note flaws). Don't question the manuscript as a whole. You're not editing; you're reading.

Now, here's the hard part. Try to "watch yourself" as you read. (Oh, sure. And try to watch yourself as you swing that wood on that 350-yard dogleg.)

As you watch yourself, note which words you skim because you know they're there. You breeze over "raging" in the phrase "raging fire," because all fires rage, it seems, and this one does, too. In this cliché, "raging" is invisible; you take it for granted. You don't think about it. Replace it with something that does work ("inferno" is far more evocative than "raging fire"), or take it out (maybe "fire" by itself will do).

But more important, watch yourself on a larger scale. Monitor your reading involvement with the material in front of you. Do you slog through certain sections? Are you reading others with delight equal to that with which you wrote it? Do you find yourself grinding to a stop five words into a paragraph, thinking "oh yeah," and leaping to the next paragraph?

At this point, the fact that you're familiar with the text becomes an advantage. Note which sentences, which paragraphs, which pages you skim. These are your trouble spots. If you, the person most interested in your writing, aren't held by certain passages, perhaps your reader won't be, either. Again, revise or eliminate.

Then—and this is the tricky part—pay attention to those phrases and paragraphs you savor, those you reread while congratulating yourself. Those are trouble spots, too. Are they too clever, too flashy, too pretentious. Maybe they'll attract the reader's attention, too—away from the flow of what you've written. That increases the manuscript's mental length.

Consider mechanizing this reading step: Retype your manuscript.

That's blasphemy, I realize, in the day of the word processor, but retyping allows you to put the "interest" editor to work quite literally on a hands-on level. When you find that the retyping is a chore beyond the physical, you have perhaps discovered more cuttable material.

Ask, Can I distill the manuscript to its essence? Can you compress it into a glistening diamond?

Manuscript compression can take place at levels both large and small. The small: compressing a couple of sentences into one, such as I describe on page 48 in chapter two. The large: compressing a number of sentences or even paragraphs into the swift and efficient.

Compressing sentences eliminates "joist" words — words you need to hold the structure of the sentence up, just as a joist holds a wall or a ceiling up. The taller the wall, the more joists you need. Restructure so you have smaller walls and fewer joists, and you save words and increase clarity. For instance, in an early draft of this book, I had written, "It's a roundup article listing the various ethnic groceries in Cincinnati, one of which is run by Tony." Tuck "Cincinnati" into another spot in the sentence, directly modifying ethnic groceries, and I draw the subordinate clause beginning "one of which" closer to the groceries it's referring to: "It's a roundup article listing the various Cincinnati ethnic groceries, one of which is run by Tony."

Compressing larger units such as scenes and settings removes the number of walls you need in the first place.

I've discussed compression on the small scale. On the large scale:

• Compression can be as simple as sidestepping the details. For example, paraphrase and summary are effective compression techniques, if they aren't made to be dense or lecturish. You can eliminate much unneeded detail with swift, general description, such as with this fiction passage:

> "Hi, George," I said, shaking his hand.
> "Fred, good to see you." His grip was firm but friendly.
> "How are the kids?"
> "Good, good. Yours?"

And how are the dogs and the houseplants and have you solved that mildew problem in the bathroom yet? Let's get *on* with it!

Get on with it with paraphrase: "As we shook hands, George and I exchanged pleasantries."

Here we've eliminated material that has failed the "so what?" test. But it's also a good way to eliminate long explication of important material — for instance, when you find that you must repeat exposition already known to readers, yet unknown to characters within the story. In Sinclair Lewis's *Elmer Gantry*, the title character, in trouble because of a dalliance, seeks the help of a friend:

> "T.J. They got me."
> "Yuh? The bootleggers?"
> "No. Hettie. You know my secretary?"
> "Oh. Yuh. I see. Been pretty friendly with her?"
> Elmer told everything.

In three swift words—"Elmer told everything"—Lewis brings Elmer's friend up to date, moving the story along without slowing the story*telling*.

• Compression can be a matter of moving some details offstage. For instance, your protagonist doesn't have to do everything. Farm out some of the job and let it take place offstage. In your mystery, must your detective track down who belongs to license KYY 304, or can a flunky in the detective's agency do the work and get back to your hero later?

• Compression can involve reduction to essence. Here's an excellent example of compression at work, as described by Paul Darcy Boles in *Storycrafting*:

> The first draft of my short story "Sweet Chariot" was not lean and uncluttered; it was twenty-four pages long. It was all there, complete, making its point without shouting at the reader; but it was also too leisurely in rhythm, and self-indulgent when it came to halting the forward motion and giving the reader a guided tour of scenic wonders and outside appearances of people. At one juncture, its main character was described as if he weren't inhabiting a *short* story at all, but happened to be in a roomy Sir Walter Scott sort of novel: "Journey was a looming, rangy man with the high cheekbones of middle Appalachia, descended from hunters, ballad-singers, keepers of their own secret counsels. His eyes, the color of very good, sun-faded denim, sometimes held hints of wild-

ness—of wanting to rush away, like a deer startled from dreaming." This is passable character-drawing, but it stands by itself without any kinship to the quick, demanding music of character-in-action called for in a short story. It's a trifle show-offy, like a set piece meant for recitation rather than reading in silence. In the process of cutting the first draft from twenty-four pages to ten, it was thrown out without a qualm. All that remained in the final draft was: "His eyes held hints of wildness and rushing away." That line does the job, summarizing everything in the original windy passage and allowing the story to move on without hanging fire.

Some of the trimming has come in stripping the description down, removing the mention of the high cheekbones and the color of the eyes. But the core of the description, the eyes, is first identified and then compacted. The hint of wanting to rush away becomes a hint of rushing away.

• Compression can involve combining major elements of the manuscript (combining two scenes into one, for instance), so that the details remain, but how they are conveyed becomes more efficient. Compressing such major elements saves setup and introduction time, which in turn saves both space *and* mental length. In fiction, for instance, you can compress your story by:

√ Combining characters. In fiction, maybe one of your spear-carriers can carry a couple of extra spears. For example, suppose you compress the bartender who reveals a choice bit of information to the protagonist into the neighbor who runs a few needed errands through the course of the story, you have eliminated the need to introduce that second character, describe him, and give him a distinct existence.

You've also eliminated potential for confusion. *The guy with the scar—is that the bartender or the neighbor?* One fewer element for readers to keep track of.

√ Combining scenes. John and Paulette argue about money in chapter two, about the kids in chapters three and five, then exchange snipes about their marriage in chapter seven. Do you really need four arguing scenes? Perhaps the arguments start small and build to a whopper in chapter seven. But if the scenes simply establish tensions between John and Paulette, maybe the exchanges about the kids in chapters three and five can be compressed into one scene. Maybe these four scenes are really one big argument that should take place in a single scene, if pacing and plot development allow it to happen in so self-contained a fashion.

√ Combining settings. John and his best friend George meet periodically at work, at the racquetball club, over sandwiches at the park, occasionally at each other's home. Stage the conversation that takes place during the racquetball scene instead at John's house, and you've eliminated the need to describe a new setting, not to mention the props (racquets and sweatbands and goggles) and such that go along with the setting. Similarly, transitions to and from that particular setting are expedited if readers have been there before.

√ Compressing time. James Grady's book *Six Days of the Condor* became the movie *Three Days of the Condor*. Tell your story over a shortened period of time, and you eliminate a few glances at the calendar or consultations with the watch.

Ask yourself, Can I put it in English? There's a little of the smart aleck in me when I say that. "It would please me if this meets your standards." *Put it in English.* "I hope you like this."

That's a broad interpretation of "put it in English": Make it understandable. But the advice is often applied literally: Likely you've been advised at some point or another to prefer Anglo-Saxon words over Latinate words (words that ultimately derive from Latin, either directly or through Latin's descendents, such as French, Italian and Spanish). There's logic to the advice. The Anglo-Saxon, because it rises from the origins of English, tends to express core concepts, concepts central to our lives, in primarily one-syllable words. "Eat," "drink," "food," "sex," "child," "food." So using the Anglo-Saxon "chew" rather than the Latinate "masticate" not only shortens what you're writing, but also allows it to resonate with the essence of our language.

Don't carry this too far, though—find me a good Anglo-Saxon word that says "rendezvous."

And the Anglo-Saxon can be terribly wordy in itself. Take the word "stick-to-it-iveness," which is kind of a garbled compound of basic English words. If we stuck to the Anglo, we'd use it regularly instead of, say, "determination" or "tenacity." Robert Claiborne, in his excellent *Our Marvelous Native Tongue*, tells the story of Reginald Pecock, an English Bishop who in 1450 sought to purify English by discarding Latinate words in favor of words with "pure" English roots. "Instead of 'impenetrable,'" Claiborne writes, "he proposed the Old English-style compound 'ungothroughsome'; another suggestion was the monstrous 'not-to-be-thought-upon-able.'"

Such compounding regularly leads us to incoming words, such as, well, "incoming"—words that are *coming into* the language. "Ongoing" is one such word, though it's decried by language watchers. "Ongoing" hardly offends me. First, it features unique meaning. "Continuing" is a close but not exact match. "Continuing patrols," for instance, suggests to me that the patrols began sometime in the fairly recent past, and they're continuing. They continue *from something*. "Ongoing patrols" suggests that the beginning is hazier, that the patrols have always been there, or at least have a longer history than "continuing patrols."

Second, and most important, "ongoing" was constructed using word-creation mechanisms so ingrained into the language that we might call them "traditional." Patrols go on; they're ongoing. And we use similarly constructed words daily. We pay income tax. We have fun with our outgoing friends. We wonder about the outcome of football games.

Remember, the more specific the word, the more clearly, the more succinctly, you communicate. Welcome any word that brings more-specific concepts to the language.

This leads to another shortening strategy that I'll slip you under the table and ask that you never say you heard it from me. Alter the question from "Can I put it in English?" to "Can I put it in something that sounds like English?"

Granted, it's blasphemy to some: If you can't find a short word that performs the function you need performed, make one up. Or give an existing word a new job. For example, you might find that using a noun as a verb might keep your sentence trim and active. "Get in contact with Fred" becomes "Contact Fred." The watchers will frown on you if you use "contact" as a verb, but, as with word compounding, such conversions have a grand tradition: Using "contact" as a verb is itself an example. The *Oxford English Dictionary* dates its first use to, oh, a few years ago. 1836.

Do you want to turn someone into an idiot? Idiocize him. I've seen accusations that people have *politicized* events. That's more efficient (though less accepted) than saying that people gave events political meaning, or that they injected political impact into those events (even though "politicize" has been around since 1856).

Can't find a word for that smug laughter deep in your throat? Lewis Carroll decided it wasn't quite a chuckle, because there was something of a snort to it. It was, he told us, a "chortle," a concocted word now accepted as part of the language because of its specificity, distinctiveness and usefulness. It says what no other word says. Comedian Rich Hall in more recent times brought us "sniglets," itself a created word describing created words — "any word that doesn't appear in the dictionary, but should." How, for instance, can big business function without "execuglide" in its vocabulary? ("Execuglide" means "to propel oneself about an office without getting up from the chair," possible only with chairs on rollers, however.)

There's nothing wrong with such snigling. This is a democratic language. Everyone has a vote. And the words that are used are those that are "elected" to use, the ones everyone chooses to use. Language by, for and of the people. Every word is a made-up word. Someone had to make it up at some point. Everyday people make them up, leaders make them up, *writers* make them up; Shakespeare gave us, by one estimate, nearly two thousand new words, including "dwindle," "obscene," "lonely" and "majestic."

A couple of created words lurk in this book. I speak of "extraneity" (the condition of being extraneous), confident that readers would understand it not just from the construction of the word but also from its parallel with "spontaneity." It's so much more streamlined than its real-life counterpart: "extraneousness." (I won't tell you what the other created word is.)

Play mad scientist with the language only with these caveats in mind:

• Do it confidently, and without apology. There are so many words in this language — some dusty yet dormant, some obscure but not obsolete, some archaic yet active. Who's to question every coinage, or even be aware that the unusual word you've just used is your coinage? If you're timid, you can set the word off with parentheses, which is a way of saying, "Yeah, I know it doesn't exist." Or you might introduce it by saying something on the order of "what we might call extraneity." But often you don't need such signals of apology.

• Don't do it often. You're seeking to streamline reading, not slow it by filling it with the unfamiliar (*Finnegans Wake* and "Jabberwocky" notwithstanding).

• Don't be cute about it. (I once referred to "editor-quette" in a book of professional etiquette for writers, and am still sorry for it.)

• Be aware of the grammarians out there who will dismiss you for not using "proper" grammar. You're less likely to attract their attention if you play mad linguist in informal writing.

Apply the "SURE" test to big words. Joe Floren in his *Write Smarter, Not Harder* presents what he calls a "SURE" test for big words:

• Is it *simpler* than a small-word equivalent? For instance, "beginner" is simpler than "tyro," "frivolous" easier than "inane."

• Is it *unique*—the only way to say the idea? Many technical terms qualify, as do nontechnical ones such as "civilization," "religion," "government."

• Does it add *richness* to your writing? To "write like you talk," you must write in a way comfortable to you. Some of those rich, interesting personal words will be large ones.

• Does it provide *economy*, taking the place of several words? That usually benefits the reader.

If it passes the test, use it. But Floren estimates that 10 to 15 percent of the big words used by the typical writer are used out of "unchallenged habit," and will fail his test.

Turn to outside testing. Have others review your manuscript. The others can be human—other writers, editors you know, teachers. Or they can be nonhuman—grammar and style-checking software. There are advantages and dangers to each.

• Human reviewers discriminate. They notice their pet peeves, they point out errors that aren't errors, they try to encourage you to revise according to their conception of what makes good writing—which likely differs from your conception, or from that of an editor who might buy the work. Or, worse still, they point out nothing, because they like you, and don't want to hurt your feelings.

• Nonhuman reviewers don't discriminate. They spot "errors"

according to set rules and definitions that can't take context, tone, rhythm or other elements of writing into consideration. They spot redundancies by rote, usually at the level of words and phrases. They can't tell you when you've told that same anecdote three times, and they can't tell you five examples is a little much in making a minor point.

Or they inspire paranoia. I once used a grammar-checker on a manuscript in which I wrote the phrase, "My wife is a pharmacist...." The robotic checker diligently pointed out that "wife" was gender-specific. Well, my wife is gender-specific, too. I understand that the software was trying to help me avoid misusing "wife" in generalizations, such as "All doctors and their wives are invited." But if I didn't understand that, if I were to pay too much attention to the software, I might end up writing stiffer phrases like "My spouse is a pharmacist."

Keep in mind, too, that grammar-checking software is often directed at an audience of business writers. Good if you're a business writer. Bad if you're a playwright.

With both human and nonhuman reviewers, take their comments as suggestions only. They can provide that "fresh eye" on your material that you often need, but *you* should be the final judge of the material. You know its purpose best. You make the decision. (Until you're overruled, of course, by that objective outsider who will pay you money to publish the writing—the editor. Even then, however, you should maintain a strong though reasonable voice in determining what is changed.)

There's another reason to not depend on reviewers human and non too much—they provide a false net beneath you. You rely on their analyses and lower your own guard. Never allow that to happen. You miss out on two opportunities: the opportunity to improve the manuscript in front of you, and the opportunity to improve your skills that you will apply when writing the *next* manuscript.

One quick thought on using the human's "fresh eye": Give your manuscript to someone who will criticize. And prepare yourself for criticism. If you give a manuscript to a reader expecting praise or confirmation, you're setting yourself up for surprise. And if you get that praise or confirmation, you might not be getting the instruction you need.

And a few quick thoughts on using the computer's "fresh eye":

• You can customize style-checkers to identify concision problems you know afflict you. Short of buying a style-checker, you can employ your word processor's search function as a kind of style-checker. One of my first editors pointed out to me that I overused the word "it." (A concision problem? With a word so short? Yes — if readers don't know what the heck "it" refers to, they have to backtrack in the copy. The trail I've given them may be shorter, but if I make them walk it again and again, they travel much farther than they have to.) I and my computer now watch for it — "it" being my predilection for "it." When I've completed a manuscript, I'll ask the computer to search for *space-it* (so time isn't wasted identifying "sit" and "fit" and so on). At each occurrence, I examine "it" to be sure its use is clear.

I similarly search manuscripts for occurrences of "that," which can often be deleted when it's understood, and of "will," as I will often fall into the future tense when it isn't needed, as I did in this very sentence.

• If you use one of those programs that counts the number of times you used individual words, ignore the frequency of common words (Oh my heavens! I'm overusing "the"!). Do pay attention to multiple occurrences of vague words ("thing," "stuff"), adverbs, adjectives, gaudy attribution ("hissed," as in "He hissed . . ."), and pronouns (a lot of hims and hers might signal that you need to be more specific in places to avoid confusion).

• Pay a little attention to those analyses of the number of words in an average sentence. If the average number is 312, you might have a problem. Still, I generally ignore such analyses. Sentences are not two-by-fours; their worth cannot be measured by tape measures — or by electronic bean counters and bean multipliers and bean statisticians.

When I was editing *Writer's Digest*, I received a letter from a writer who had analyzed some WD articles with software that counted the number of words and sentences in a manuscript, the number of words using three or more syllables, and other such factors, and determined a "readability index." The letter writer claimed WD was unreadable, more or less because the computer told him it was. That reminded me of Writer's Workbench, one of the first editing programs. In 1981, *Discover* magazine tested the opening sentence of the Gettysburg Address with Writer's Workbench, and revised it according to the program's suggestions. The result:

Eighty-seven years ago, our grandfathers created a free nation here. They based it on the idea that everybody is created equal.

Has a certain lilt to it, doesn't it?

And when the opening sentence of *A Tale of Two Cities* was similarly scrutinized, this paragraph resulted:

The times were the best and worst, wise and foolish. The era was one of belief and disbelief, light and darkness, hope and despair. Before us lay everything and nothing. We were all going direct to heaven or straight to hell. The period was so much like today that its loudest critics could describe it only in superlatives.

Writer's Workbench then crunched a few numbers, and reported that a typical reader would need 46.1 years of education to understand the original version. Best get yourself back to school soon if you want to read Dickens in the original anytime within the next three decades.

Measure your writing in words, not numbers.

• Finally, grammar software can help you become aware of problems that plague you. But I think you'll outgrow the software after a few uses, and it will become more irritant than instructor. Kind of like a parent still correcting your pronunciation even after you yourself have kids.

Word-processing technology will continue to improve and surprise, and to provide you with electronic ways to monitor your prose. For instance, I cannot inject into my manuscript the nonword "t-e-h," because the moment I type those letters as a discrete word, a dictionary function I have programmed converts it to "the." I could similarly program the dictionary to convert some word I misuse frequently into the word it should be. Say I've fallen in love with, for instance, "utilize." I could ask my fancy dictionary program to replace it with "use" every time I typed it. Or, if I inject "basically" into my sentences, um, basically too many times. My ever-vigilant dictionary could replace it with the more appropriate empty space; it would delete it.

Dangerous is the technology that takes decisions out of your hands (not to mention your head), however. I would prescribe such autoconversions only for the most severe problems, or you'll find yourself unable to write "basically" when "basically" is the right word, to write "utilize" when *it* is the right word.

But despite the faster-than-lightning growth of technology, do you know what improves faster? what surprises more? *Your own abilities at the keyboard.* Depend on them. Depend on the quantum leaps that occur in your head.

Decimate your prose. More accurately, "tricimate" it. On a photocopy of your article, or, preferably, in a backup computer file copy, delete every third word indiscriminately. Put the copy aside and come back to it in a couple of days. If the manuscript makes any sort of sense after your random chopping, it was pretty flabby to begin with. Return to your original and evaluate each word.

Now, go through the first draft of your manuscript and eliminate every third paragraph. Return to it in a couple of days. Is the flow making any sense at all? If it does, chances are you're spending too much time in unnecessary explanation, example or transition.

Rewrite blind. Here's something you might try once or twice to see if you find it useful. Put your manuscript aside and forget about it. Then, tackle it again fresh in a few hours, or a couple of days. Put the original phrasings out of your head and write a portion of it from scratch—the lead, perhaps a description from the middle, maybe a set of conclusions from near the end. Consult your notes if you want to, but beware: Your notes might be the source of the problem. Notes rapidly jotted aren't honed, streamlined, expressed in the best way possible. Translate notes as if they were a foreign language; don't copy them verbatim. (I discuss the dangers of heavy reliance on notes on page 78.)

Then compare new and old versions. Maybe the blind rewrite will point to ways you can improve the first: You defined that concept in fewer words the second time around, that bit of dialogue has less attribution and fewer exchanges but works anyway, and so on. Maybe the rewrite is an overall improvement, and the first draft can be totally replaced. Or maybe you'll be pleased to find out you did it best the first time.

Or—and here lies a danger—maybe they're both good. You defined a difficult concept well the first time through; the second time, you employed different metaphors and came up with an equally interesting and useful definition. Do not be tempted to include both. Choose one.

Avoid the "Danger Signs of Wordiness." Big topic, this one, and an important one—which is why I've devoted the next chapter to it.

5. The Danger Signs of Wordiness

A security guard pauses on his rounds when he sees a strip of tape across a door latch.

Something's wrong here, he thinks, and months later a president is toppled.

A writer pauses as she reviews a manuscript when she sees a prepositional phrase beginning with the word "of."

Something's wrong here, she thinks, and moments later an entire sentence is toppled.

An overblown analogy, I grant you. Comparing preposition abuse with abuse of presidential power is extreme, and I promise to never again compare anything so serious with something so seemingly common as crooked politics.

The point, though, stands. A little thing out of place—a piece of tape or the preposition "of," as thin and common as a piece of tape—can signal larger problems. Pause on your rounds through your manuscript when you see the following little things out of place.

Where there's smoke, there's fire, yes? Usually, but sometimes where there's smoke, there's someone grilling ribs over glowing coals in a smoker. No fire, no danger. The smoke is there for good reason. So, none of these danger signals is absolute. I warn against footnotes, for example, but not all footnotes are bad. Try to present a research paper without referential footnotes.

It's like the difference between a tornado warning (tornado sighted) and a tornado watch (conditions are right for the formation of tornados). Most of the other chapters of this book constitute a wordiness warning; this one constitutes a wordiness watch.

Conditions are right for the formation of wordiness when you see:

Commas; semicolons — dashes: colons. Consider these punctuation marks as sharp stones on a rocky road. Writing cluttered with such punctuation guideposts is likely to be choppier, more convoluted and lengthier than writing that can be presented without them.

(Parentheses.) Or, worse yet,[1] Parentheses and footnotes often introduce digressions. Deal with digressions in one of three ways:

* *Delete them.* Even if they're interesting, they can misdirect attention, or confuse the reader. *Why are you telling me this?* the reader thinks. *How is it connected to everything else?* Digressions not only inflate a manuscript, they give it a misleading apparent range of coverage.
* *Move them.* Perhaps digressions can be isolated into a self-standing sidebar. Maybe they provide the core of another manuscript. Send 'em packing now; invite them back when you sit down to prepare your next project.
* *Redefine them.* Perhaps they aren't digressions after all. If you don't want to delete or relocate the material because it is indeed important, perhaps a slighter trim is in order. Don't delete the parenthetical material. Delete what classifies it as parenthetical material: the parentheses. Placing material in parentheses diminishes its perceived importance; so does dropping it to the bottom of the page in a footnote in smaller type, the typographical equivalent of whispering in the theater while the movie plays on. So consider restoring it to its proper position in the text by removing the parentheses, or by booting the footnote back up into the primary text.

Parentheses and such do have their place, as I mentioned above about the footnotes. Parentheses are used, for instance, to offer further explanation, as I used them earlier to help me define the differences between a tornado watch and a tornado warning. Here the material within is not superfluous digression, but instead needed elaboration or extension.

Pay particular attention to parentheses in fiction. Author intrusion or obtrusive exposition is often lurking between them. For example:

That night Bob packed his bags and took a bus to Racine,

[1] Footnotes.

Wisconsin (a town of 75,000 about thirty miles south of Milwaukee, along Lake Michigan).

Perfectly acceptable explanatory use of parentheses if that passage appeared in a nonfiction piece; clumsy exposition in a novel.

Wordiness. Granted, saying that wordiness is a warning signal of wordiness is somewhat like saying a bear sitting in your lap may signal the presence of bears in the area. I mean that one instance of wordiness may signal other instances nearby. A proofreading rule of thumb is to increase your guard for typos whenever you spot a typo. If the typesetter was tired or distracted enough to let one typo slip, he or she probably let other typos slip during the same stretch, for the same reason. Typos travel in packs.

So do redundancies and their cousins. If you let your guard down long enough for a passive to creep in, perhaps the door was open long enough for a tautology to creep in behind it. When you spot one, search for the rest of the pack. If in the following example, for instance, you had stopped at removing one bit of verbosity, you would have missed an opportunity to trim the sentence even further:

Wordy: Be sure the program you buy is current enough to meet your needs.
Better: Be sure you buy a program current enough to meet your needs.
Keep Going: Buy a program current enough to meet your needs.

Telltale phrases. Serial criminals often leave behind clues that the criminologists and cliché-makers call "cries for help"—the criminals, by leaving such clues, demonstrate that they want to be caught. Your prose can leave behind such blatant cries for help, in the form of clue phrases, which include:

• "But, to get back to the story, . . ." Why did you ever get away from the story in the first place? Backtrack to find where you went astray.
• "By the way, . . ." This has all the earmarks of, "As long as you're traveling to Cleveland, you might as well stay a day or two in Columbus." Columbus is, literally, "by the way," but if a Columbus

sojourn has nothing to do with your getting to Cleveland, consider skipping it. So, too, the section introduced with "by the way," "you may be interested to know that..." and so on. Such phrasings are verbal parentheses, in that the material that follows them is parenthetical, tangential, to be handled as I advised above.

"Thursday's finance committee meeting has been rescheduled for Friday. By the way, Thursday is the slowest day of the week for me, so for those of you who participate in my weekly production meeting, let's hold it Thursdays at 2."

Two memos for the price of one. Delete the by-the-way material and move it to another memo, one that will be read only by those who participate in the production meeting. Stay on the way; don't pause by the way.

• "In other words..." If you need other words, why did you use those words in the first place? Just use the right words, and the right words only. "In other words" can sound condescending, as if it means, "OK, for you idiots out there who didn't understand me the first time..." Variants include "What I mean to say is..." or the seemingly quiet "i.e."

On the other hand, perhaps you indeed need those other words. They elaborate on or further explain your point. In that case, they are additional words, not "other" words in the strictest sense, and you have a different opportunity for trimming. Just chop out "In other words," and let the points flow together.

• Such phrases as "needless to say," "as you know," "of course," "obviously" and "it goes without saying." Well, if it goes without saying, then let it do so. Some of these phrases do have function. They tell the reader you're not a dope. "The man said I could have either a can of tomatoes or $200,000 in cash. I obviously took the cash." That second sentence is really saying, "I'm no dope. I took the cash." But beware describing the obvious in the first place, and labeling it so in the second.

• "As you can plainly see..." If it's that plain, you don't have to draw a conclusion about what the reader has seen. If it's not that plain, don't insult anyone by saying that it is. If you insist on using this phrase as a transition, at least boil it down to the less wordy "As you see..."

• "Let me digress for a moment." Requesting permission to waste the readers' time doesn't make it any the more acceptable. Nor does apologizing after the fact: "But I digress..."

• "I'll get straight to the point." Indulge my cliché: "Actions speak louder than words." What better way to prove to the reader that you'll get straight to the point than presenting the point and skipping the throat-clearing?

• Phrasings such as "As mentioned before," "As described above," or "As I'll detail in a moment." These can signal that you've scattered related information if not to the four winds then at least to your own windiness. Perhaps the related information can be drawn together to be discussed once, efficiently.

Numerous adverbs and adjectives, especially strings of adjectives. "I said loudly." Perhaps you yelled. Or shouted. Most adverb-verb constructions can be reduced to single, more specific verbs. Similarly, many adjective-noun constructions can similarly be reduced to more specific nouns.

Not all adverbs come wagging their "ly" tail. They won't bite, nor will they bark. But they do get underfoot. For example, "We knelt down before the alter." The adverb "down" modifies "knelt"— to no apparent purpose.

Watch out for these adverbs, among others:

• "Up." There's as much closure in "We closed for the night" as in "We closed up for the night." Another example, quoted from a memo in my in-basket this morning: "The author continued to shape the book up until his death." Out with the ups.

• "Down." There's that kneeling business, as one example. As another, "drop down," redundant because you can't drop up. You *can* drop in, out, over, by, back and off, but these are not part of the core definition of "drop," which is to fall.

• "Over." "Pass the bread over to me." Drop the "over"; better to underuse it than overuse it.

• "Together." If we blend things together, are they better mixed than if we simply blend them? If we gather people together, are they a better group than if we just gather them?

• "Behind." As in "following behind" (as opposed to following in front of).

• "Out." For example, "My 'yes' vote and her 'no' vote canceled each other out." The out is unnecessary. Cancel it, too.

And watch vigilantly. For instance, I kicked off the list of adverbs to watch for by saying "Watch *out*." Don't watch out; simply watch.

Adverbs of whatever stripe of course have their place. They're useful when:

• They communicate two distinct thoughts, or the verb-adverb combination can't be boiled down into a single word. For example, "He studiously ignored his father." We're all familiar with the idea of theatrically not noticing something. But we have no word for that concept.

• They work. You could argue that "ice cold" is redundant. There is no warm ice. But I contend that drinking a glass of cold water is an experience different from drinking a glass of ice-cold water. One is simply colder than the other.

Numerous prepositions. They fly about like gnats, those ins and outs and ofs and such, bothering readers. Swarms of prepositions can signal wordiness.

Take "of," for instance. It's a quiet little word that does enormous work, some unnecessary. "Of" can signal one of two opportunities for tightening:

1. You can often convert "of" constructions to possessive formations:

"The report of mine is on your desk" becomes "My report is on your desk."

Not that I'm suggesting that we revise the title of the classic song "House of the Rising Sun" to "The Rising Sun's House." Here we're losing rhythm and emphasis at the least, and at the most, clarity. And, as with "House of the Rising Sun," some "of" phrasings are so common that altering them would be distracting and, considering the space saved, ludicrous.

You can similarly convert the object of the prepositional phrase (the prepositional phrase's object?) into an adjective preceding the noun the prepositional phrase describes. Lots of grammar talk there meaning you could convert "roll of film" into "film roll" ("film" is the object of the prepositional phrase modifying "roll"). Such conversions can also be awkward. "Roll of film" is common and invisible—

"film roll" is unusual. On the farm, you could say "hay bale," but "bale of hay" is more common. And you would never consider converting "Hall of Fame" into something shorter.

Other prepositional constructions can provide similar signals. If appropriate to context, clarity and sentence rhythm, "the man *from* Cincinnati" becomes "the Cincinnati man" in much the way as "the native *of* Cincinnati" becomes "the Cincinnati native." "The team *out of* Pittsburgh" becomes "the Pittsburgh team." "The city *in* Alabama" becomes "the Alabama city." "The book *about* concision" becomes "the concision book." "The novel *by* James Michener" becomes "the James Michener novel."

2. You can eliminate chatty, roundabout sentence construction. Take, for instance, a sample business sentence, "We will proceed with implementation of the plan." Converting it to a possessive form trims it, slightly: "We will proceed with the plan's implementation."

But the "of" here has signaled an even larger problem. An active verb, "implement," has been converted into a stagnant noun, "implementation." Revert it: "We will implement the plan."

The "of" in this example is not cause but merely symptom of this weak construction—which is becoming more and more a problem, especially in business writing. The "of" construction allows you to link a weak verb (discussed in more detail on page 39) with a mutation of the verb that should drive the sentence (I discuss such mutations further in a moment)—in this case, weak verb "proceed" with verb mutation "implementation."

Prepositional phrases allow you to distance important words from other words they should be directly connected to; they even allow you to hide important words. And sometimes they allow you yourself to hide. "I'm in favor of the plan" is less committed than "I favor the plan."

"In" can signal some egregious problems: green in color, rectangular in shape, soft in feel. Green is a color, rectangular is a shape, soft is something you feel—why identify them as such?

Words like "nature" and "manner" appearing in prepositional phrases signal particular problems. For example, "Report in a timely manner." Better to say "Report on time."

The dangers of this construction take a variety of forms. There's the unneeded reflexive descriptor:

He worked at a leisurely pace.
He worked leisurely.

There's the noun converted to adjective:

He got a hit of the line drive variety.
He hit a line drive.

There's the empty tag:

The note was congratulatory in nature.
The note was congratulatory.
Better yet: The note congratulated (him/her/them).

There's the jury-rigged adverb:

He tossed the book to the floor in cavalier fashion.
He tossed the book to the floor cavalierly.
Better yet: He cavalierly tossed the book to the floor (which brings the adverb and what it is modifying together)

Related, there's the modifier torn from its home:

Such phrases signal writing of a verbose nature.
Such phrases signal verbose writing.

Some prepositions aren't signals; they're just plain unneeded:

Meet me on Thursday.
Meet me Thursday.
Beware of the dog.
Beware the dog.
Both of these examples . . .
Both these examples . . .

Verbs converted into nouns. Shun the "-tion," as in "infla*tion*." Specifically, word inflation. Which results when you perform conversions on verbs and make them nouns (or, more succinctly, when you convert verbs into nouns). Return such verb-based nouns to their roots to strengthen your sentences.

Take, for instance, the object of this sentence: "Give the plan your concentration." "Concentration," of course, is formed from the verb "concentrate." Send it back to its roots, and you can write "Concentrate on the plan." In an early draft of the first chapter of this book, I wrote that I would *"point out the correlation between* the living art of the bonsai and the living art of a well-shaped, well-pruned manuscript." I revised that to say I would *"correlate* the living art..." Think of a sentence as a car. A '69 Mustang. Now, saying "point out the correlation" is like putting a Yugo three-cylinder under the hood and storing the 360 horses in the trunk, where they just weigh things down even further. In this case, "correlate" is the engine, and I hooked it directly to the drive train.

Gerunds—verbs converted to nouns using the suffix "-ing"—can present similar problems. "In a well-written script, each character contributes to the advancing of the plot." Better that each character contributes to "advancing the plot," stripping out "the" and "of." Better still that each character "advances the plot," dumping the weak and wordy "contribute." When possible, zing the "-ing."

When you spot "-tion" and "-ing" verb-conversions (as well as other types of formations, such as "decision" or "conveyance"), scan the rest of the sentence. Chances are you'll find a weak verb close by—"do" or "make" or one of several others I discuss starting on page 39. A classic example of this is "We're in agreement." That awful, quibbling sentence features three warning signals: the gnatty preposition, the weak verb "are" (hidden in a contraction, yet), and the verb-to-noun conversion.

Overabundant similes like ivy underfoot. Similes are like ground ivy. A little in the yard can be pretty, but too much can tangle your feet.

A simile is a figure of speech comparing two unlike things using the word "like." "Similes are like ground ivy" is itself a simile. (Metaphor is similar, but more direct, as well as bolder and riskier. Metaphor states that one thing *is* something else, not that it's *like* something else. "Similes are ground ivy" is a metaphor.)

The potential tangle of similes comes in two forms:

1. Similes come out of a mold; each is structured like almost every other. The sun is like a red rubber ball. The fog is like a blanket. Blank is like blank. Blank is like blank. (Note, too, that it's easy to slip into cliché in this simile template.)

2. More direct to the focus of this discussion is a concision tangle. Lurking in the usually useful simile is the weak verb "to be." Blank *is* like blank. That's passive comparison.

Avoid overdependence on similes by using other tools. For instance, let's say we have just written, "I lay on the bed. The mattress was like concrete." We can tackle the sentences these ways:

- Tighten them slightly and become more direct with metaphor: I lay on the bed. The mattress was concrete.
- Take the metaphor a step further and recast the sentences so we don't even mention the mattress: I pulled back the covers and lay on the concrete beneath them.
- Compress the sentences and turn "concrete" into an adjective: I lay on the concrete-like mattress.
- Compress and take even more license: I lay on the concrete mattress.
- Compress by converting the second sentence into a subordinate clause: I lay on the bed, the mattress concrete beneath me.

By now you've caught me. Two of the above examples are longer than the original sentences. But they are more direct, and as sentences are better reading conduits.

"I." When you walk into your prose, you risk directing the attention away from your subject. Perhaps you have a place in the prose (see my discussion of "the self-indulgent" starting on page 51 to find that place). But when you see "I," raise your antennae. If you don't belong in the manuscript, get out. And if you do, don't wear that loud tie.

6. Exercises for Developing Your Awareness of Concision

*I*n a different career, a different city, a different geological epoch, I studied theater. My acting instructor taught us an exercise that has served me to this day. Try it yourself:

Lie on the floor or on your bed. Close your eyes; get comfortable.

Now, concentrate on the section of your left thumb between the knuckle and the tip. Tense just that portion of your body as hard as you can for ten seconds, then release it. Now, tense the entire thumb for ten seconds; release it.

Add your left forefinger. Tense thumb and forefinger; release them. Add your middle finger, your ring finger, your pinky. Then tense the entire hand and release it. Add your left forearm. The entire arm, your leg, the limbs on your right. Continue adding, tensing, releasing until you tense your entire body, hard, for ten seconds before releasing all your muscles.

This exercise helped us actors identify tense parts of our bodies before going onstage; once we isolated the tension, we could release it, just as we had released it in the exercise.

I gave up the stage but kept the relaxation exercise, which I found useful in handling deadline pressures, staying relaxed while sitting for long stretches at the keyboard, and so on. In time, though, I saw that the exercise applied to the mental act of writing as much as it did the physical. Tighten your writing the way you tightened your muscles, tighten it until it hurts, until it is hard and taut—but also unusable because it's inflexible. Writing can't be as tight as an actor's muscles in a relaxation exercise. Writing must flow as smoothly as an actor's movements before the lights.

Tight is "That's the problem of which I spoke." Loosened is "That's the problem I spoke of." And, strangely enough in that

example and often in writing in general, the loosened is shorter than the tight.

So, use the following exercises not as the knife you apply to your manuscript, but as practice for becoming proficient with the knife, and learning when your cutting and tightening have gone too far. You'll also learn the value of loosening up, of letting writing flow as the actor flows across the stage—with no wasted movements, without stumbling. (It was that stumbling part that got me out of theatre, I suspect).

Run with weights strapped to your ankles. Figuratively, of course. Make it physically hard on yourself to get words on paper. If you compose easily at the keyboard, spend an hour writing longhand. If you can't type, hunt and peck an hour's work. If you're good at both, write a few pages in a bulky crayon, or write left-handed if you're right-handed . . . just make it difficult on yourself physically so that your mind tries to make it easy on you mentally. Your mind will begin to find ways to alleviate the task, to lessen the work, to take shortcuts. The shortcut you're looking for is the one that uses the fewest words, yet communicates the messages.

Digest some digestibles. Writer Joe Mooney in his *Seattle Post-Intelligencer* column referred to *Reader's Digest*'s condensation of the Bible as "the Gospel according to Tonto." *RD*'s condensations are ripe for parody and jokes (and I've taken advantage of that ripeness myself, I'm afraid), but the *Digest* folks are good at what they do. Learn from them. Ignore the jokes about the Reader's Digest Condensed this or that and compare, page by page, sometimes paragraph by paragraph, sentence by sentence, a Reader's Digest Condensed Book against the original published version. Or look up the original publication of an article reprinted (and often condensed) in *Reader's Digest* magazine. Note what is lost other than the words. Note also what is gained.

Listen to sportscasters and do the opposite. OK, that's the cynical side of me speaking. Not all sportscasters mangle the language. Every once in a while a Vin Scully or a Bob Costas comes along and uses the language respectfully and with occasional eloquence. Yet, they say the best sportscasters are those who have played the game, and I contend that we should get a few that have played some word games, some journalism games, in addition to the ball games. (Consider Harry Caray: "The groan is audible. It can also be heard." Or Curt Gowdy: "He was originally born in Chicago.")

So let's change this advice to "Listen to how language is misused all around us, and learn from others' mistakes." Jot down the redundancies and verbosities you see and hear; create your own "glossary of the redundant," such as the one starting on page 185. If you write it down, you'll be more likely to remember it later. If you hear someone say "The two are united as one," jot it down.

For that matter, listen to yourself, especially as you speak. Everyone is prone to verbal padding while talking; note the padding you and those you speak with employ.

Once your antennae are up, you'll hear and see dozens of examples of language obesity. On the radio just moments ago: "I know I may be beating a dead horse to death." *That* would do even the Spanish Inquisition proud. When you spot it, relish it. But do more. *Apply* it. Yes, you've discovered still another example of wordiness, but the lesson is not in the particular example. In this book, I've tried to give plenty of examples, but more important is my attempt to show how those examples represent general principles. When you spot wordiness, analyze why it's wordy.

Walk a mile with my red pencil. Take a piece of writing — not one of yours — and play editor. Your assignment: Reduce the word count by one third without disrupting meaning. If it's 3,000 words, take it down to 2,000. Don't expect to do it all at once. Go through it several times over a period of four or five days, tallying the words you slice out. You'll see something different you can cut on each pass through the manuscript. Perform this surgery on about five manuscripts, and you'll see more specifically the types of extraneity that can be trimmed, and you'll come to appreciate that there's very little writing that can't be cut.

Compare the printed version of a manuscript you've sold with your submitted version. Implicit in many cover letters accompanying submitted manuscripts is a request: "Teach me a few things about writing." It's an unrealistic request. Editors are paid to do many things; teaching is not one of them.

Yes, editors can and do educate. They can help shape careers just as they shape manuscripts. But aside from the occasional comment or tip dropped into a letter or flagged on the margin of a manuscript, they educate only in the doing, in the editing. They work to get material into print. If you watch them at work, you can pick up valuable skills that you might never pick up from someone whose only job description is "teacher."

The classroom here is the manuscript itself. The teacher, ultimately, is you. You teach yourself by comparing what you submitted against what was printed, and asking, Why was that change made? Was the writing too wordy? Had I slipped into cliché? Was I straying from the point?

Such comparison has two definite benefits, not the least of which is learning the lesson that even though you're a published writer with published-writer check in hand, you still have things to learn. The other benefit is, of course, you see your own writing through the eyes of a pro. You spot what he or she spotted and that you missed (or saw but liked)—and you learn to spot similar problems as you write your next manuscript. Perhaps you'll learn to spot it, and stave it off, before that particular problem hits the page in the first place.

You'll get some of this instruction from the editor if he or she asks for revisions. "You tend to spend too much time getting to your central point, especially in the second chapter." Use it. Sometimes the instruction is more specific. "This metaphor on page 17 is labored." An isolated problem? Be honest with yourself. Perhaps you should work on your metaphors throughout the manuscript, throughout your writing.

Pay attention to such direct advice. Pay as much if not more attention to the indirect advice in the editing. Here's where the editor works hard, last leg, end in sight, to get the piece ready for publication. Here's where attention is paid to detail, and matters of concision often lie in the detail.

Of course, editing is not necessarily good editing. Too many editors out there should be learning and not teaching. Still, bad editing can lead to good learning. Even if you disagree with how your writing was changed, try to discover why the change was made. What problem was the editor trying to address, even if he or she bumbled in addressing it? Identify problems, and come up with your own solutions.

What did the editing of this book teach me about concision in my own writing?

• I learned that I use "a bit" and "to a point" and "in and of themselves" too much.

• I learned that I would use punctuation to emphasize what words had already made clear, and vice versa. This sentence, for example: We shouldn't trust supposed "experts." The quotes around the final word, and the word "supposed" both communicate that they're not really experts; no need for both.

• I learned a lot of other things I won't bore you with or embarrass me with. But most important I learned the need for vigilance. The phrase "unneeded verbiage" slipped through several readings by different people before I caught it late in the process. There's not much *needed* verbiage.

Relive the "Good Old Days." Be your own editor, your own teacher. Go back to something you wrote a year or more ago. A poem, an article, a short story, a chapter of a novel. Read it, then ask yourself not How good is it? but How tight is it? You'll likely spot four or five words a paragraph that could have been left out. This won't show you so much *how* you can improve your tight-writing skills, but that you can in the first place. You'll gain the confidence that comes with knowing you're improving, and that you can continue to improve. The "good old days" of your writing is now, and knowing you will improve, they will be "gooder older days" as you practice your craft.

As an example, let's look at one of my good old days: the introduction to *Professional Etiquette for Writers*, written in 1986.

> Like water and electricity, agents, editors, writers—everyone you'll ever come into professional contact with—seek the path of least resistance. Simply put, they just don't want to deal with unnecessary fuss and falderal.
>
> Given the choice between two clients with equally good books, an agent will choose the one who is reliable, friendly, courteous and professional over the one who's moody, argumentative, lackadaisical and generally a pain. . . .

That's enough. It was good enough to get published, but it could have used work. I already see these little problems:

• "Ever" performs no function.

- Not much "fuss and falderal" is necessary.
- "Simply put" is condescending padding.

There are others. But let's move to the larger problems:

- If the concept can be simply put, why didn't I put it simply in the first place?
- The fourth item in each list describing types of clients — "professional" and "generally a pain" — summarize the previous three, and could be deleted.
- The second sentence is a mouthful. Today I might write those sentences something like this:

> Like water and electricity, agents, editors and other professionals you'll work with seek the path of least resistance. Given a choice between two clients with equally good books, an agent will choose the reliable, courteous and professional writer over the moody, argumentative and lackadaisical one.

It still doesn't sing, but neither did the first version — and the second gets to the point far more quickly.

Linger at the dictionary. This advice bears repeating. Yes, look up the words you can't spell as you write and those you don't understand as you read. Examine the words' origins, as I recommended with "pedal." And here the advice bears extending: Look up more than meanings and origins. Look at what some might call the "gestalt" of the word: its complete list of meanings, its evolution, its gene pool, what it used to mean. Taste the nuance of the word. Absorb it.

When you're done with that word, spend time with another. And another. Look up three or four words every time you pick up the dictionary. Taste and learn. Similarly stroll through the thesaurus and other word books. The larger and more precise your vocabulary, the easier it is to write succinctly. But as we've discussed: Vocabulary is a tool, not a badge; use it as such.

Guard Your Vocabulary the Way You Guard Your Pocketbook. This isn't a technique, but something of an attitude: I like what Kathryn Lindskoog says in *Creative Writing: For People Who Can't Not Write*: "I suggest to students that they pretend they have to pay me one dollar for each word they use, to see how many dollars they can save if they try." They'll save a lot more—by having a lot more dollars paid by editors—if they pennypinch their words. A word saved is a dollar earned, depending on international verbal-financial exchange rates, of course.

Make a Game of Concision. Not a frivolous game. Not a pastime. Something you have fun doing. Play, but play constructively.

In nature, the play of young animals precurses the "jobs" they will perform later in life. Cubs and kids and maybe even goslings practice being adults in their play, rambunctiously and harmlessly applying the skills that will help them survive when the time comes for them to care for their own young. Bear cubs wrestle, kittens stalk and pounce, children play Scrabble. These games tell bears how to defend themselves, cats how to hunt for their food, and people to, well, babble a lot. Which seems to be a very human survival mechanism. You think you wrote on your eleventh-grade English final that "Shakespeare evokes a sanguine articulation of pre- and post-posterous proportions" because that's what you *meant*? You were trying to *survive*, and wrestling the teacher to the ground in a bear hug just wasn't going to work.

We reward big words from the very start. We ooh and aah the precocious child who spouts big words. We have spelling bees that reward those who can spell the big words, but no parallel competition that rewards those who know what the heck they mean. And we have Scrabble. Form that big word with the X's and the J's and score big points. Great fun, and about the only opportunity you're going to have to use "reticulation" in public. The Russians came along some fifty years later with a computer game variation called Wordtris. Letters drop from the sky (manna from heaven?) onto a placid water surface. You control where they land—plop them in the right place, and you form words. The bigger, the better. More letters, more points.

In an odd way, we communicate to kids that when they play with big words, they are practicing their own survival tools. We then allow them to think that big words mean survival in the adult world—because often it does. As adults, we pursue emotional survival when we hide behind fluffy euphemisms by saying someone's contract hadn't been renewed instead of saying he was fired. We elevate ourselves when we speak of sanitation engineers instead of garbagemen (or garbagewomen). We dodge the tough questions with rambling answers that at the least give us more time to think our way out of the situation and at the most give us a complete smokescreen we can escape behind. Survival through linguistics. With big words we impress, disguise, and move ahead. Or so it appears on the surface, and as I've discussed elsewhere, quite the opposite is true.

Don't get me wrong. I have nothing against instilling large working vocabularies into our kids. I have nothing against spelling bees. I have nothing against Scrabble. But do keep in mind that good writing is kind of Scrabble in reverse. Lay down fewer letters, score more points. Or as Wordtris in reverse. Boil the letters out, float them away, score more points. More points with the reader, that is.

Make a game of concision; make it fun. Make it important, but make it enjoyably important. The best professions, after all, are the ones you have fun doing.

7. Reducing the Mental Length of Your Manuscript

I've spoken often in this book about mental length. Material that is mentally long might be physically short, yet it slows the reading experience, because it's difficult to slog through. Such material hinders readers with, at best, murky translucence; at worst, opacity.

Or, maybe the material just *seems* difficult to slog through.

As I've mentioned before about reader perceptions, it doesn't matter if your writing is breezy and quick or ponderous and glacial. What the reader thinks it is is what it is. And the following types of material are ponderous and mentally long, perhaps because they are, or perhaps because readers think they are.

Material that feels long includes:

Lectures. My four-year-old puts his hands over his ears when I launch into a loud, strident monologue about cookie consumption or some other indiscretion common to four-year-olds. Your readers aren't much different from my Kevin. But unlike me, you can't watch your audience tuning out, allowing you to raise your voice accordingly. You lose your audience, hands over ears and eyes, invisibly. *You* must avoid lecture. *I* must hide those cookies.

Lecture can slip in from two sources: You the writer can lecture, or lecture might bubble up from within the writing, from the people speaking in your manuscript, whether fictional characters or real sources.

Sometimes the lecture is defined by the *intent* of the writing: to drive home a point, somewhat relentlessly, without leaving room for argument or disagreement. Pomp and pontification.

Sometimes it's defined by *form*, which is why I advise to beware the long continuous quote in nonfiction *and* fiction. No one speaks in soliloquy, so if readers encounter four paragraphs of uninterrupted speech, pontification or no, they perceive it as contrived. *No one,* they think, *speaks that articulately at such length.* They're probably right. You lose verisimilitude, you lose credibility. You also foist on the reader a slowdown of action. One person talking means that nothing else is happening. If the speech is interrupted, at least by some verbal response from other characters, you introduce dynamics into the scene.

Summaries. The "tell" part in the important writing adage "show, don't tell" refers to summary. The "show" part is usually action in fiction, demonstration and example in nonfiction. Two rules to keep in mind here:

1. Don't use summary to replace showing. Summary is shorter but more difficult to endure—not to mention just plain less interesting. Would you rather watch Hitchcock's *North by Northwest* or listen to your friend tell you the plot, with lots of *and then*'s thrown in? Would you rather read *The Old Man and the Sea* or have me explain that Santiago had gone a long time without catching a fish, but finally got a big one, and fought it for a long time at great physical expense, *and then* the fish was eaten by sharks near the end of the book?

2. Don't tag showing with telling—don't summarize what you've just demonstrated (unless, of course, the form of your writing demands such summary, as with an academic paper).

Summary is deadliest in storytelling forms: fiction, narrative nonfiction, scriptwriting (having characters tell each other what they've done, or that script scourge—the explanatory voiceover). In informational materials, summary is often not only acceptable, but also crucial.

Hype! Hype is *hard to read*!!! I once reviewed a book manuscript submission THAT USED A LOT OF ALL-CAP SENTENCES!! Not to mention EXCLAMATION POINTS!! I felt tired by the end of the first chapter. So, DON'T DO THAT!!!!! Resort frequently to caps and exclamation points, throw in *italics* and **boldface** and other visual "shouters," and you lend a feeling of hyperactivity that makes the writing harder to read. Besides, if you must resort to exclamation points and the like to make your point, the words themselves aren't doing their work. Two exclamation points side by side look like the crutches they are.

OK, avoid the exclamation points. What else? "You are about to read the most astounding tale of concision ever told on this planet." Wow! Tell me more. Better yet, tell me less. Don't get my hopes up with promises and self-congratulatory stroking. Granted, I've given you an extreme example. Here's one that's not so extreme: "Followed properly, the advice I'm going to give you will save you 20 percent on your next car purchase, guaranteed." This isn't as tiring as picking your way through the barbed-wire fence of exclamation points, but it still adds to mental length because your reader is likely to regard it skeptically.

Material that unnecessarily raises questions in readers' minds. If you're writing fiction or certain types of nonfiction, keeping the reader in suspense can be good. Suspense — what's going to happen? how is this going to turn out? — draws the reader through the prose, *because the reader wants to be kept in suspense.* Suspense is integral to the fiction; enduring suspense is integral to the fiction reader.

But in purely informational writing, don't keep readers in the wrong kind of suspense. Don't delay conclusions or your point. Present the important stuff first, the support stuff later. This is the organizational style known from the newspaper world as the inverted pyramid. In journalism, it's what happened — "Two people were killed in a four-car pileup on I-90 outside Beloit yesterday" — followed by what led up to its happening. In business, it might be asking what you want, then explaining why you want it. Or it might be stating your conclusions, then following with supporting evidence. If readers agree with your conclusions, they can skip or skim the supporting evidence — or choose to read it carefully anyway. You've put the choice in the readers' hands. If they want more or need more, they'll pursue it. If they don't, they can move on. Either way, you have served your purpose; you have presented your point efficiently and concisely. Reverse the order — present the support information before you present your conclusions — and readers begin thinking, *What's the point of all this? Where is this leading?* Those questions will tend to dominate the readers' minds, not allowing them to concentrate on the specifics of the support information you're presenting.

I'm reminded of a recent real estate dealing. My wife and I were discussing an offer to buy our house with an agent. For fifteen minutes the agent ran through sales charts listing sales of comparable homes; for fifteen minutes, I regularly said, "Fine. What's the offer?" I couldn't concentrate on the charts while I was trying to figure out what the charts portended. In informational writing, don't portend. Explain.

Another way to keep readers in the wrong kind of suspense is making provocative statements or claims without explaining them right away. For example, on page 173 I give this advice: "Retype troublesome parts [of your manuscript]. That's a moot point if you still work on a typewriter—you're likely to retype *everything*, and that's good. . . ."

The flow of the chapter dictates that I explain why you should retype troublesome parts before I explain why you should retype *everything*, so if I simply jump into the "troublesome parts" thing, I would have readers saying to themselves, How the hell can retyping *everything* possibly be good? instead of paying attention to my other points. To eliminate the lingering question, I add a simple phrase: "for reasons I'll detail in a moment." By saying that, I tell the reader, "Forget about it for the time being, because we'll be back to that." I eliminate a distracting suspense.

Consistently long sentences and repetitive construction. I've made the point that long sentences aren't evil in and of themselves, as long as they are clear and readable. But if every sentence is long, if you lay length end to end to end, the readers' impression that the entire manuscript is long will increase. This is more a function of repetition than of actual length. In fact, strings of short sentences increase the mental length of your manuscript almost as much as strings of long ones. So do strings of anything cloned, whether the cloning is of sentence construction (subject-verb-object, for instance), or of starting every sentence with the same word ("George did this. George did that. George did the other thing"). A manuscript consisting only of similar building blocks is a meal consisting only of dishes made of broccoli. Good individually; tiring and difficult to stomach in total.

Vary sentence length and construction within paragraphs, and paragraph length within the manuscript itself. (For a fuller discussion of this, see pages 138 and 139.)

And a Few Smaller Brambles

Foreign phrases. They are difficult to understand sometimes, *nicht wahr?* Nicht *what?* Even supposedly common foreign phrases can slow readers down. For instance, *C'est la vie,* such is life. This is commonly understood, perhaps, in speech. But for the French-impaired, such as yours truly, on paper it looks not like the *Say la vee* we've heard so often, but like the last syllable of "incest." And thus, we are confused.

Dialect. "Regionally foreign" phrases, as it were. Dialect doesn't show up as much in fiction these days, which is good. "Ahll be a-collectin' a canna carn fer da ev'nin's' sup." I don't know what that says, and *I* made it up. If you want to demonstrate regional speech in fiction, hint at it with colloquialisms, with altered cadence and grammar, and the occasional altered spelling (such as "collectin' " for "collecting," and the like). Stay away from wholesale phonetic transcription. Just as with foreign phrases, readers can't "hear" dialect by reading odd spellings. They decipher it. They can, however, hear it through the *rhythm* of the writing.

In nonfiction, the dialect you "write" will come out of the mouths of your sources. Even there, keep dialect to a minimum. Yes, quote your sources accurately. But that doesn't necessarily mean reproducing their grammatical variances and spelling the words they speak phonetically on the page. So what if your source said "Warshington D.C."? If it illuminates a point about the source—her education, her regional origins, whatever—fine. But if the point is "Washington D.C." and not how the name of the city is spoken, spell it traditionally. Let the reader concentrate on the point, not on weird spellings.

Numbers. Too many of us have trouble with numbers. Years ago I attended a football game. A fan near me asked his friend: "How long to go for a first down?"

"About half a yard."

"It can't be that long," said the first fan. "It's about two feet."

Or how about this, heard on a recent sports broadcast. "The team has won three games in a row and is now four and oh on the season."

Parade those numbers past the readers, and you slow them down for two reasons: First, they confuse many people. Even the simple ones above confused people. Start talking about percentages of increase per capita pro-rated over fiscal quarters and you have all but those who understand such numerical argot saying, "Huh?"

Explain what the numbers mean—explain their impact on the reader. Because, after all, numbers support your point; they are not the point. That's true even of business communications—say, a sales report. OK, so we were $200,000 over budget in sales in February and $75,000 under in March. What does that *mean*? Perhaps it means that we budgeted sloppily and should change the procedure for next year. Perhaps the month-to-month fluctuations are part of a pattern we must adapt to. Perhaps it means the sales director should start looking for other work.

Material—such as a book chapter—presented entirely in checklist form. Which is why I'll take the opportunity to end this chapter.

8. Nonverbal Streamlining

*W*riting tight involves more than leaving out words. It also involves *laying out* words — laying them out on the page, the physical presentation of your writing.

How the words are laid out on the page affects how the readers perceive those words. If they fit well together physically as well as logically, they give the impression that the entire piece of writing is constructed well. If the doors on the car you're considering buying fit snugly, you tend to think the whole car is built well.

This relates to my point on page 7 about appealing to reader perceptions. You can deliver writing that is truly tight and well honed, and you can deliver writing that the reader *perceives* is tight and well honed. The ideal, of course, is to deliver both, in the form of writing that is concise in both construction and presentation.

Thus the importance of the elements of physical presentation we will discuss here, because you can use these presentational tools to not only trim material but also indirectly point out how trim the material is in the first place.

You as a writer have little control over how words are physically presented to the readers. Editors and art directors and typographical conventions dictate the typeface used in the published version, as well as the type size and the amount of leading (the space between type lines). All these affect readability, the ease with which the reader can move through the written material.

There are, however, elements of physical presentation you *can* control, elements that contribute to readability. Initially, and on a purely mechanical level, this means submitting clean manuscripts, avoiding typos, and otherwise following commonsensical manuscript-preparation guidelines. But that work will be important only to your first reader, the editor, and not to your ultimate reader who will never know anything of your original manuscript (unless it is so good that it is archived). The physical elements I'm talking about are those that translate in the design and editing process into printed type. These elements can organize, focus, shorten, streamline and pace the material. They include:

- Sidebars
- Subheads
- Footnotes
- Paragraphing
- Checklists

Let's start with that final item, then. "Checklists" concludes what has just proven a useful tool for me: the checklist. And how can I discuss it in any way other than as an item on a checklist? Specifically, a checklist of tips for nonverbally streamlining your work.

To pick up the pace of informational material, present items, tips, instructions and other "nuts and bolts" in a checklist. Look again at the checklist of presentational elements above. Suppose I had presented it as straight-line text: "These elements can organize, focus, streamline and pace the material. They include sidebars, subheads, footnotes, paragraphing and checklists."

The first version takes more space on the page, yet *feels* more streamlined, more precise. It isolates each item on the list, and by doing so imbues everything on that list with importance. The second takes about the same number of words and conveys the same information, yet has less authority than the checklist. Or maybe I should say less "clank" to it. It's softer, more linear. The checklist is the bookkeeper's column of prose, the packing list, the itemized invoice. It seems more tangible than items in straight-line prose, even more accessible. That reduces its mental length, because it's easier to read and refer to.

And, frankly, writing lists is easier than writing prose. Think of it as painting. Lining up your jars of paint in a sequence resembling the rainbow is a lot easier than mixing them up on a canvas and ending up with the Mona Lisa.

Which is to say that there's no art in list-making, and therefore no room for it in what is traditionally termed creative writing, which in my mind includes narrative nonfiction. Remember, we're after a "feel" in the presentation, a hard edge. Checklists are especially important in material that is to be "used": reports, how-to articles, instructions and so on. The list format is good for instructions, steps in a procedure, advantages and disadvantages of a product or a procedure, and so on.

To see just what kind of edge checklists give writing, compare a spot of poetry with a spot of packing list:

> How do I love thee? Let me count the ways.
> I love thee to the depth and breadth and height
> My soul can reach, when feeling out of sight
> For the ends of Being and ideal Grace.
> I love thee to the level of everyday's
> Most quiet need, by sun and candlelight.
> I love thee freely, as men strive for Right;
> I love thee purely, as they turn from Praise.
> I love thee with the passion put to use
> In my old griefs, and with my childhood's faith.
> I love thee with a love I seemed to lose
> With my lost saints, — I love thee with the breath,
> Smiles, tears, of all my life! — and if God choose,
> I shall but love thee better after death.

Elizabeth Barrett Browning. Now, let's turn it into a checklist:

How do I love thee? Let me count the ways. I love thee:
• to the depth and breadth and height my soul can reach, when feeling out of sight for the ends of Being and ideal Grace.
• to the level of everyday's most quiet need, by sun and candlelight.
• freely, as men strive for Right;
• purely, as they turn from Praise.
• with the passion put to use in my old griefs, and with my childhood's faith.
• with a love I seemed to lose with my lost saints.
• with the breath, smiles, tears, of all my life!
• And if God choose, I shall but love thee better after death.

Now, let's make it really clank.

How do I love thee? Let me count the ways. I love thee:
1. to the depth and breadth . . .
2. to the level of . . .
3. freely . . .
4. purely . . .
5. with the passion . . .
6. with a love . . .
7. with the breath . . .
8. And . . .

Ah, a *numbered* checklist. *Now* we're quantifying (Browning wanted to count the ways). The numbers give the writing further edge, further precision, as if it has met the standards of the International Linguistic Bureau of Weights and Measures.

Checklists take a variety of forms: There's the grocery list — a simple list of items or things to do or whatever it happens to be, each item on a separate line. There's the prose list, in which the items are run together in a single sentence, separated by commas, with the final item preceded by "and." There's the numbered list, such as the one we just completed, which is a type of the prevalent "bulleted list."

"Bullets" do much the same thing to lists as numbers do. Bullets are dingbats, visual elements that set off list items. Bullets include:

1. Numbers, though they're rarely referred to as bullets.
● A circle — usually filled in.
■ A square — also usually filled in.
✔ Checkmarks.
☛ Never bullets.

They can also take the form of arrows, pound signs, or other icons, including the popular floating pointing hand ☛ borrowed from the old circus posters.

To indicate that you want list items led off with bullets, simply type a paragraph indent, then a lowercase *o*, or, less commonly, an asterisk. You might jot the word "bullets" next to the first bullet, but it's not necessary. Don't tell the editor what kind of bullets you want; few writers do that, as a designer selects the style of the bullet.

USA Today reporter Kevin Maney once extolled the bullet as presentational and organizational tool in *Writer's Digest*: "Bullets help you organize because they force you to identify the story's most important points." Also: "Bullets save words because you don't have to worry about transitions." True. The bullet is itself the transition, saying, in effect, "A related point," or "Here's something else."

What's more, Maney says, bullets help readers as well. "If a reader isn't interested in what's under one bullet, he can skip to the next." That sounds like an odd way of speeding the reading experience, giving the reader opportunity to ignore portions of your prose, yet "skippable" prose can have value in making readers more comfortable with the reading experience. I discuss this in more detail in the section on sidebars, which follows shortly.

Avoid checklists in which support material runs a number of paragraphs. The readers, immersed in what you're telling them, will forget somewhere in the middle of paragraph four that they're moving through a checklist item. When the next bullet or boldfaced head comes along, especially if that item isn't self-contained and self-explanatory, they'll have to pause to remember why it's there. "Oh, yeah. Item three on the list." With material of that length, you're better to organize the copy under subheadings (which I'll discuss further in a moment).

Or, if you want to retain the checklist feel and structure without the physical trappings of the list, employ the "hidden list," in which each item is given a separate paragraph and is discussed more loosely than strict list format might allow. For example:

> Professor Freddington claims to have discovered bits of evidence that counter the "Big Bang" theory of the creation of the universe.
>
> Most important is the discovery of . . . (etc.)
>
> The second bit of evidence, which other scientists have worked to discredit over the years, concerns . . . (etc.)
>
> Freddington's third bit of evidence is that . . . (etc.)

You can easily visualize those paragraphs as a numbered checklist, presented bang bang bang. But here they are presented with more conversational flow, allowing variations in introductions, and additional information such as the fact that one bit of evidence has provoked controversy. The prose feels looser, yet the information presented is attached to a strong organizational spine. It's a checklist

spine . . . but it's also an outline spine. You can picture some types of informational writing—especially reports and nonfiction articles— as long checklists, in that an outline is something of a checklist itself.

That might sound a little mechanical, and perhaps it is. But the outline-as-checklist skeletal model has broader application than you might first think. Fiction, for instance, can be examined in checklist format.

"This is the first thing that happened."

"This is the second thing that happened."

And so on. You just happen to leave out the "This is . . ." business, and get on with the material.

Move interesting but tangential material of a couple of paragraphs or more into a sidebar. Sidebars are stories within stories. They're used most often in newspapers and magazines, but sometimes appear in books. Turn the page for an example of a sidebar.

Sidebars have dual purposes, dual advantages. First, isolating indirectly related material in a sidebar allows the main text to flow more strongly, while the interesting side trip isn't lost. Second, and ironically, isolating the material in a sidebar lends the impression that there's more material overall than if the same text had appeared in the body of the article, that the article or whatever is more complete than it might have been. Readers perceive that the material as a whole is longer, yet more streamlined, as they know they can skip some of the material (the sidebar) if they so choose. That perception of choice is important; readers may be willing to read all the material if they feel that you aren't forcing them to do so, or that you have taken pains to organize your manuscript in a way that is convenient for them. As with bulleted material, don't let on that the sidebar is probably more for writing convenience than for reading convenience.

Again, sidebars add to informational feel. I once wrote this to the writer of a reference book I was editing (name changed to protect the excellent—this was my only complaint about the book): "I yearn for more facts and hardcore nuts and bolts. How this book will be used will determine how we should present information, and the book will be used as a reference tool. People will open it to Look Things Up. We must respond to that in two ways: 1) Help them Look It Up, by organizing material into 'look-up-able' form, whether that form is a sidebar, a chart, a list, a glossary, a chronology,

This Is a Sidebar
This material, a self-contained unit related to but not crucial to the material that surrounds it, is a sidebar. The term has its origins in printing (surfacing about 1945). It referred to a block or bar of type off to the side. Now, pausing on page 135 to examine the roots of the word "sidebar" would have put the brakes to my discussion of how sidebars are to be used. Thus, it more appropriately appears in this discreet space.

whatever. 2) Give them lots to Look Up. Checklists and sidebars and such are information-conveyers, fortifying the feel of the book as a reference tool."

Keep sidebars short so they don't attract too much attention from the main article. (Keeping the sidebar headline short will also help keep the sidebar discreet as well as discrete.) One writer suggests that the sidebar compose no more than 15 percent of the length of article and sidebar combined.

Books also carry sidebars. Try to keep them short enough to appear on a page (about 400 words of copy), or, at most, on a two-page spread (about 800 words). Longer and the reader will have to turn the page to follow the sidebar, and the flow of the material can get confusing.

To indicate material as a sidebar, start it on a separate sheet of paper and simply label it a sidebar. Number it separately, as well.

Another discreet space you can move tangential material into is a book appendix, kind of a sidebar gone mad. But do so cautiously. I've seen books whose appendices took up 30 percent and more of the text. Appendices, like sidebars, are aids. They should stand by, not stand out.

Use subheads as stepping-stones. A subhead is a smaller headline appearing within the text of a story. For instance:

This Is a Subhead
I used to hate subheads. "They interrupt the flow of the copy," I would argue. I've changed my opinion over the years, because I've

discovered that, quite to the contrary, subheads guide the flow of the copy, not only for the reader, but also for the writer. In my letter I quoted a few paragraphs back, I recommended that the writer of the reference book use more "organizational leaders," and noted that sidebars, checklists and, yes, subheads could be used to lead the organization (and writer and reader along with it).

Starting on page 87 of this book, I talk about testing your copy by jotting key words that describe the thrust of each paragraph next to that paragraph. Then, you group the paragraphs with similar key words together.

Those key words should be the stuff of your subheads. Good subheads are guideposts to the reader just as the key words were guideposts to you when you wrote the piece. That word "guideposts" is important. No one appreciates a clever street sign. Darn few more appreciate clever subheads, so keep them straightforward. Make their meaning clear, and most important, make sure they apply directly to the material that follows. And do not make the subhead more interesting or more provocative than the subject that follows it.

Clever? Never Ever

That one is borderline. It communicates a distinct, understandable thought, one pertinent to the discussion and therefore useful for reader reference. But it's perhaps too cute in its rhyme. A simpler one might have been "Never Be Clever."

How many subheads should you use? A guideline I once used when editing magazine articles was to insert a subhead about every 400 words. I now suggest that you don't watch the odometer quite that closely. Each subhead should set off and identify a clearly defined section of your manuscript, in much the same way that a sentence isolates a single thought, and a paragraph isolates a series of related thoughts. A manuscript section situated between subheads should isolate a series of related paragraphs.

In fact, step back from a manuscript in which you use subheads. Skim it, paying particular attention to the subheads. If you have organized the piece properly, you will sense a flow to the heads, you will see how they help you move, step by step, from the beginning of the manuscript to the end.

You may even begin to see the outline of the manuscript reflected in the subheads—perhaps you will even see the heads as items on a long checklist that is your article.

Get rid of footnotes. Beyond the fact that, as I covered in chapter six, the text of the footnote itself is often tangential, the physical ride jumping from the middle of the page to the bottom and back again disrupts not only the physical but also the mental flow of reading. Plus, including footnotes is a good way to assume the scholarly air, and the impression that you're not writing, but instead stiffly engaging in stuffy elucidation systems.

Set pace with paragraphing and sentence length. Looking to pick up the pace of your manuscript?

Want to give the impression of breeziness?

Even breathlessness?

Break up your paragraphs.

Something else to consider: Break up your sentences.

But if you're looking to slow the pace of your manuscript, to give the impression of solidity, even determination, present your information in solid, cohesive paragraphs, and don't consider breaking up the sentences.

Paragraph and sentence length also govern how formal the manuscript feels. Shorter, quicker clumps of words sound more informal than carefully constructed word weaves. Especially when you use sentence fragments. Like this. What I have just written is less formal than, say, if I had written, "Shorter, quicker clumps of words sound more informal than carefully constructed word weaves, especially when you use sentence fragments, which I wouldn't possibly do in formal writing."

Fragments? Weren't they burned at the stake by the Language Inquisition in the Salem Fragment Trials of the early 1600s? Some word watchers would have it so. Others have no problem with fragments; Flaubert once wrote, "The best sentence? The shortest." Just make sure that fragments pass the test any word or usage must pass:

- They must make sense.
- They must fit the style of the rest of the manuscript.
- They must be the best way to communicate what you want to communicate.

Varying length of both sentences and paragraphs not only gives you control over pace, but also makes your writing less tedious.

Subject verb object. Bum bum bum. Sentences sound like a rhumba. Step step dip. It gets boring. Boredom slows readers. Vary your pace.

"Open up the text" with "white space." That's a typographical term for any part of a page not sporting type or a graphic. White space makes a page look less imposing, less cramped.

At the opposite end of the spectrum, a page jammed full of type is called "gray" — step back from a densely packed page and you'll see why. The words blend into a single block of gray. Gray pages scare off readers — or so goes the conventional wisdom in the publication business.

Many of the elements I've described here contribute to how much white space will appear on the printed page: subheads, shorter paragraphs, organization of material into checklists. But there are other ways to add white space, as well. For instance:

You Might Isolate Important Points,
Centered,
in Their Own Space on the Page

You might use block quotes to set off long quotes, instead of running them into the rest of the text.

You might, as a writer friend of mine has suggested, "Open things up with dialogue."

"Dialogue? Why?" I asked.

"It's generally easy to read, and more personal. And . . ."

"And . . . ?"

"And it adds white space, which the readers of this book will notice in this exchange."

Rather than repeat certain types of material, cross-reference it. For more on this topic, see page 547. Just kidding.

A book on electrical repair, for instance, might early on present a checklist of safety precautions that one should take before starting any project the book discusses. Rather than repeat the precautions at the beginning of each project, you might just issue a reminder. "Before beginning, consult the safety precautions listed on page 10."

And if a topic on page 356 relates to another on page 25, a cross-reference can point out the connection, delivering more information to the reader and increasing the perception of completeness of your material.

But don't overdo it. Frequently asking readers to refer to other parts of your book or to jump to a chart or a footnote adds *physical* length to your manuscript—the distance the reader must travel flipping pages. The benefits of centralizing the information must outweigh the additional time and trouble—the mental length.

And never cross-refer to material beyond the material you are writing at that moment. Make your manuscript self-contained. Don't let the reader get into the middle of it and find out that the batteries weren't included—that something important to your subject has been left out, or is packaged somewhere else. "Refer to my book on quantum physics for the six principles of inertial energy." Talk about your inertia; who's going to stop reading the material in hand, hunt for a book or an article or maybe even a chart six pages hence, and then come back? That's not to say you shouldn't direct readers to sources of additional information, but don't *force* them to seek those sources.

Recap the needed information. For instance, in a business report, don't say, "My position on this matter was outlined in my 12/4 memo," and send everyone scrambling to their files to find a memo that has long since been recycled. Recap: "As I've previously stated, my position on this matter is . . ."

Use charts and other visual aids where appropriate. Comparisons, measures, gauges—some material lives a clearer life in visual form, perhaps as a bar graph or a pie chart. I'll leave the advice at that. This isn't a desktop publishing manual.

Import the physical conventions of other writing forms into the one you're using. For instance, looking for production-line efficiency in presenting dialogue? Turn to the stage and its script dialogue format. But remember that a playscript is a tool; it isn't the final medium of presentation to the audience. Turn to the format in print only for utilitarian purposes—transcripts, and the like—or if you seek some type of effect: A particularly chilly exchange between people who dislike each other, for instance, might be made even chillier using script format. But you will almost never use such stagecraftery in narrative, whether fiction or nonfiction. It has all the poetry of a court transcript.

Mix and match formats, as appropriate. Primarily, I'm thinking of using the checklist or the Q&A as a sidebar. This allows you to isolate *information* that might be in the spirit of the main piece, while the *style of presentation* might be at odds with that of the main piece. For instance, after the prose/checklist format I've set up for the bulk of this chapter, I wouldn't want to jar you with a format switch.

> **Q:** What kind of format switch?
> **A:** Say, moving from a list of checklist instructions to a Q&A format.
> **Q:** Why would that be jarring?
> **A:** Well, I've set up one kind of pace, and a Q&A uses quite another.
> **Q:** Is that bad?
> **A:** Yes. Especially when the switch in formats is as self-consciously cute as this is.

Now, suppose I list that little *Q&A* exchange out of the main text and make it a *sidebar*? That way, the two presentation formats don't conflict; the physical separation of the sidebar puts it at slight psychological remove from the main text, so its physical format needn't be consistent with that text.

The Danger of the Devices
When using these tools, though, beware their potential dangers, including (oh, heck, let's use a checklist):

• Condescension. Feeding information in carefully measured spoonfuls can belittle readers and their ability to comprehend standard English sentences. It can also demean you and your ability to put together those sentences.
• Telegraphy. "Tip: Use concrete word. Stop." You can lose control of the pace of your manuscript if you put yourself too much in the hands of physical presentation.
• Nonwriting. "That's not writing," Truman Capote once said of Jack Kerouac's work, "that's typing." A similar charge can be leveled against overuse of these tools. "That's not writing. That's organizing." And though organization is a crucial component to good writing, it must not be the only component. As Art Spikol once wrote in his *Writer's Digest* Nonfiction column, "The Q&A format is a trap. It sets

its own limits, and they're absurd: why would any writer set out to write an interview-style article that would restrict itself to the words that are spoken?" He blasts the Q&A as "the easy way out"; the other devices I've discussed here can supply similar easy ways out. Don't, for instance, be tempted to fade off to a checklist in a prosaic piece just because you can't think of a better way to make a series of transitions.

This is especially true in fiction. Beware fiction checklisting: The protagonist walks into the room and notes every item, one by one. "A microwave on a cart stood near the door. Four chairs sat around the kitchen table; one was a high chair. A window was above the table. To the right was an open pantry that contained four brands of cereal, some macaroni and cheese, cooking oil, Cheez Whiz...." Another character comes into the room, and the protagonist sizes him up, top to bottom, listing his hair, facial features, size of neck, set of shoulders, shirt, belt, pants, shoes.

Granted, these "checklists" are prosaically presented, yet they are nothing more than packing lists. "Your fiction should contain one microwave near the door, cart; one kitchen table, four chairs (one high); one pantry (Cheez Whiz included in model 778-A14)...."

The minimalist fiction of the late 1980s was often dismissed as checklist writing—its practitioners were said to resort to listing the contents of a character's kitchen cupboard or quoting what was on a character's T-shirt rather than doing the hard work of characterizing through traditional means.

These devices, and the other devices quoted here, can pace your writing, but they can also brand it. Used to extreme, they can move into that category of forms that seem like work to read.

Use them, but with reserve, and finesse.

9. How Tight Is Too Tight?

*I*n my bonsai-trimming zeal, I've unfortunately killed a couple of my trees. Too many branches off, too many leaves, and I ended up with one sleek, compact, dead bonsai.

As with bonsai, you prune manuscripts to make them thrive, not make them die.

So, just because you haven't trimmed your words to the bonsai bone doesn't mean your writing is flabby. Long sentences and big words are not in and of themselves bad for your manuscripts. For example, one of my favorite words is *sesquipedalian*, formed of two Latin roots: *Sesqui*, meaning one and a half. *Pedal*, meaning of the foot. Loosely translated, "one and a half feet long." It means, in English, "wordy." How wonderful to have a wordy word describe "wordy." How wonderful to have a word that is in itself a foot and a half long (or thereabouts) to describe such a concept. It is a mouthful word, a wordy word, the right word.

The documentation of an early version of a grammar-checking software program noted how it would allow you to simplify sentences such as "We will reprimand the culprit." The documentation claimed that the software would figuratively ring bells and blow whistles and otherwise alert you to your sesquipedalian writing, and suggest that "reprimand" could be replaced with "punish." The helpful program would allow you to save a whopping three letters. Noble. And well worth the inconsequential side effect that the entire meaning of the sentence had been changed. "We will reprimand the culprit," with its implication of written or verbal warning, perhaps some sort of suspension, has meaning far different from "We will punish the culprit," with *its* implication of severity, perhaps even incarceration, deprivation or violence. The right word is the right word.

Wordy writing and flabby writing similarly aren't synonymous. If you need a hundred words to fully communicate your message, use each and every one of the hundred.

We seek concision to serve precision. And, ultimately, we seek concision to preserve clarity, flow and readability. So, when wordy works, be wordy. When long works, go long. Go ahead and be a sesquipedalian rapscallion—if it serves the writing.

Look at concision as a necktie. Oh, do you look good in that crisp white shirt and that paisley tie. But if you're going to do any huff-and-puff writing, writing that works and sweats, stoops and lifts, or maybe takes a swift hike or dances a bit, you'd better loosen that paisley, or you'll get all red in the face because the blood just ain't flowin' through that bottlenecktie. Sometimes the tie is uniform of the day. Sometimes you'd better have a jogging suit.

Former St. Louis manager Whitey Herzog, with opinions as straightforward and level as his flattop haircut, once commented on why so many modern baseball players, supposedly more fit and highly tuned than any generation of players, injured themselves so easily. Pulled hamstrings, bruises, you name it. "They should eat more red meat," he said. Put some fat on, he said.

Whitey's diagnosis and prescription: Being too healthy can be bad for you. Something you're supposed to avoid can be good.

Writing whose muscles are too taut, lacking a degree of body fat, can similarly pull up lame in its dash to first base. So avoid pulling your writing muscles; loosen things up in these writing situations.

When tight writing robs the manuscript of rhythm. "Now, Dasher! now, Dancer! now, Prancer and Vixen! On, Comet! on, Cupid! on, Donder and Blitzen!... Now dash away! dash away! dash away, all!" That's a lot of ons and nows and dashes and a lot more fun than "Hey, reindeer, let's blow this pop joint."

When tight writing misdirects emphasis. In the introduction to this book, I noted that concision is "crucial to the impact of your manuscript." I considered revising that to read, more succinctly, that concision is "crucial to your manuscript's impact." But I found that by doing so, I diminished the power of "impact." By taking "manuscript" out of the prepositional phrase and converting it to a possessive, I introduced it to the reader sooner, putting it into the spotlight sooner, and slipping the spotlight away from "impact." Subtle, yet important enough to prevent me from revising the sentence.

When tight writing draws the form of the writing away from its content. Form should match content. Short and snappy is an acceptable goal if you're presenting information or telling a short and snappy story. But if you're telling a more expansive story, perhaps more expansive prose can be excused. Sometimes it's crucial.

Sentences need not be built according to blueprints and building codes. They can flow, like rivers, like jazz. And sometimes they should. In my short story, "A Moment in the Sun Field," I wrote this about a boy about to catch a fly ball, "The ball spun, and began to fall, and Bobby positioned himself under it, held his glove out not for a whole ball, but just a piece of one, because it looked like just a piece of one, a slice of ball, the slice splashed extra white in the high sunlight." That's a conglomeration of thoughts and fragments that, with sentence building codes in mind, one might be tempted to break into distinct sentences. But all that must go into one sentence, because everything there is related, is part of the single "moment" of the title. It is a long moment, an important one, and communicating the action in a series of shorter sentences would have dissected the moment.

When tight writing reduces clarity. As Kathryn Lindskoog says in *Creative Writing: For People Who Can't Not Write*: "If the first virtue of good writing is clarity, the second virtue is brevity." Lindskoog means to emphasize the importance of brevity, but ultimately she appropriately reminds us that brevity is subordinate to clarity.

Here's a quick example: "I put the ball on my nose and spun it."

Sure, that's shorter and less repetitious than "I put the ball on my nose, then spun the ball." It's also a lot funnier, with the potential confusion over what precedes "it." My nose, I assure you, cannot be spun.

Penny wise, pound foolish; syllable wise, manuscript foolish.

If you must explain something, take the time to explain it. If you don't, you disserve the reader. At best, you add mental length in the form of confusion; at worst, you mislead readers.

Tightening should reduce fat, not cut muscle.

When tight writing changes meaning. I referred to the differences between "reprimand" and "punish." I once saw a copy editor change "People are judged on what they accomplish" to "People are judged on what they do." To me, these are wholly different concepts. You can do a lot of things without ever accomplishing anything.

Tightening should focus meaning, not change it.

When tight writing is just plain wrong. In today's paper a headline tells me, "Catholic Church shifts as priests dwindle." Oh, sure, the headline fits the space, but I picture these poor shrinking priests, looking rather like the irradiated hero of *The Incredible Shrinking Man*, trying to peer out over the pulpit as their shoes mysteriously get roomier. The headline writer meant to say, "as *the number of* priests dwindle." But to shorten the headline, the writer shortened some priests.

Headline writers seem wont to give us lessons about forced and harmful tightening. Associated Press style—the guidelines most newspapers use to govern spellings, comma use and other such matters—once asked that headline writers use "cigaret" instead of "cigarette" and "employe" instead of "employee" in headlines because they are shorter. AP style would also allow me, should I have written any of the previous as a headline, to use 'single quotes' instead of "double quotes"—again, because of the space-saving involved. Me, whenever I see single quotes in my daily newspaper when double quotes are called for, I look out the window and expect to see Big Ben. That's how the English do it, after all.

More than just the headline writers are to blame, though. Witness the inroads that such words as "nite," "lite," "thru" and "tho" have made in recent times (though they seem to have backed off, perhaps to make another charge soon). There's little sense in defending any of these usages, though I've come to accept "thruway" as a vaguely legitimate word, only because converting to "throughway" would frankly confuse people who understand the unique meaning of this new (birth date 1943) word, "thruway." And that oddly correct "wriggle" is slowly and, I believe, appropriately being replaced by "wiggle." (Is "indict" soon to be replaced by "indite"?)

Granted, you're not out to tighten by slicing out individual letters unless your stock in trade is the classified ad (6 rms rv vw), but the principle translates to other sorts of "knee-jerk" trimming. For example, streamlining zealots love to light on "utilize." "Wordy! Wordy! Just use 'use,'" they say. Well, sometimes "utilize" is the right word, when used in its sense of putting something to a use other than the one it's intended for. When you use a fingernail file to saw a bagel in half, you are utilizing the file. (But when you say something like "He utilized the toothbrush to brush his teeth," you are utilizing "utilize" — putting it to other than its intended use.)

Is it "wrong" to say, "I *used* a fingernail file to saw a bagel in half"? Perhaps not. But it is less wrong, and more accurate, to say "I utilized a fingernail file . . ."

When tightening is done inconsistently. Follow through on your cuts and changes. Consider how any change you make will affect the rest of the manuscript. If, for instance, you used "his or her" in your first draft and want to change it to a more succinct "her," make sure you catch all the "his or her"s, or you'll distract readers.

When tight writing feels longer. An optical illusion I saw a number of times in my grade school days involved placing two boomerang-shaped pieces of cardboard side by side, so that the convex outer edge of one was near the concave inner edge of the other. The one on the left was clearly the longer of the two. But take the one on the left and place it on the right, and the one now on the left looked longer. Then take either one and place it on the other, and both were exactly the same size.

Optical illusions of a sort can occur in writing, in that writing that's too tight and too dense can *seem* longer than looser text that actually is longer, because dense writing is more difficult to maneuver through. An example in the physical world: two hundred yards of jungle is "longer" than two miles of desert. That's one reason narrative description is longer than summary description, yet seems shorter. (This is discussed in detail in chapter seven, page 124.)

When tightening eliminates "voice" or "style." These are what makes you sound like you. And writing that has eloquence and "voice" often seems trimmable, but with a snip-snip here and a snip-snip there, it becomes textbookish. Readers are interested in more than efficiency when reading. So don't trim the beauty marks along with the fat (and remember the occasional appeal of "love handles").

Let's go back to a point I was making on page 26 of this book — *and to the way in which I made it.* Don't flip pages; I said:

> While hooking up my son's Nintendo (yes, I bought him books that Christmas, too), I disconnected the cable input

from the TV, making the screen as fuzzy as my son seems to be when he plays Nintendo. "Did you pull the wrong wire, Dad?" he said with typical six-and-a-half-year-old confidence in my grasp of electronics. "You're not supposed to do that."

I peered at him from the wire web parlor that the electronic spider had invited me into. I said, "Can you think of a time when you *are* supposed to pull the wrong wire?" I may not be able to beat him at Super Mario World, but I have a slight edge in that language-use game for the moment.

Now, I could have boiled that down to something like, "Once while hooking up Nintendo, I pulled a wire that sent the TV screen blank. 'Did you pull the wrong wire?' my son asked. 'You're not supposed to do that.' I replied, 'Can you think of a time when you *are* supposed to pull the wrong wire?' "

Boy, that's a whole bunch shorter. And, to my mind, it's a whole bunch drier, and less effective in setting up and delivering the tartness of my reply. Most important, though, is that there's a certain, shall we say, "wrongness" to the second version, given the context of this book and its author. The first version is me. The first displays my voice. The second does not. Does that really matter to the reader who might be saying (maybe *you* said it), "Get *on* with it"? Yes, in that the second version, feeling almost alien to me, would make me somewhat uncomfortable while writing it. That brings us back to a writing tenet I ascribe to—"The more you enjoy writing something, the more the reader is likely to enjoy it."

Do *not*, however, rationalize an anything-goes attitude by claiming that it contributes to voice. "I vas yust followink orders—der vuns I got from der Voice." Because there's also another writing tenet I ascribe to: "The sentences that please you most are the first targets for cutting."

How do you balance those two tenets? I'll give you the same advice I'd give a high-wire artist. Stay in the middle, and don't step off to either side. That's another important part of developing voice: avoiding the self-indulgent. If you step back to admire something you've written, if you feel *real* good about it, examine it closely to make sure that you are admiring good communication, writing that serves the topic and the reader, and not superfluous exercises in flash.

Remember that voice and style should be quiet. They are not established with gimmick. When you strive for voice and style, you don't achieve it. You simply show off.

When tight writing reduces atmosphere, connections, insights, nuance, flavor—all those elements that contribute to the richness of the writing. If, that is, richness is of value to your manuscript. Fiction and poetry demand richness. Narrative nonfiction depends on certain levels of richness for its effect. The business letter? Keep the richness out of it.

Fiction, especially, is a type of writing in which you fill in soil so things can grow instead of excavating away the earth to reveal long-dead, fleshless skeletons. Fiction, to me, is the art of making connections. Plot is one event connected to another. Theme is one idea loosely connected to another. Story is fact connected to character connected to setting (connected to the kneebone . . .). To make connections, fiction must contain connectors. It must be full; it must be rich. I once told a writer in a letter:

> In a novel I've been noodling for some time, I needed an unusual barkeep, and in creating her I gave her just three fingers on one hand. No reason, other than to make her distinctive. But by the end of the first chapter, I let her do some of the talking, and she explained how she had lost two fingers, and very shortly the loss of the fingers became important to the plot then unfolding. Including reference to the three-fingered hand was, in a sense, sowing a seed that I harvested—by making certain fictional connections later.
>
> Many beginning writers sow no seeds. They include no detail, or if they do include detail, it is for the sake of description or verisimilitude. It is rarely done with the intent of creating a few layers that might be mined later. The mining might be done in terms of plot, or of later expanding a characterization, or of creating a voice, or of weaving connections throughout the fiction. Because in order to weave connections, we must have a stock of proper connecting points.
>
> Had I written that first scene sparingly, had I left out a detail here and a detail there, I would have been robbing myself of connectors, ways of establishing relationships and ties that more than added to my plot; it *created* it.

The idea of connectivity applies to other types of writing, as well:

• Humor. To avoid burrowing into a long discussion of what makes something funny, I'll resort to a quick oversimplification: Humor is often the art of surprising people by pointing out how two seemingly disconnected things are somehow connected. Two quick examples. "The pun is the lowest form of wit," but it is the clearest form of example. Puns connect things simply because the words that describe them sound alike. Or, as another example, a riddle: "What's the difference between men and certificates of deposit?" Two radically different things are being contrasted. (The difference? At least CDs mature.)

• Poetry. Some poetic devices are driven by their ability to communicate one thing by connecting it with something else. Analogy is connection; symbolism is connection.

• Nonfiction. The best nonfiction describes people, events or procedures in terms of "What this means to you as the reader." So there's the matter of connection between subject and reader, but that's not what I'm talking about here. Meaning often comes from connection. An upcoming Presidential election. A stagnant economy. The actions of the federal bank governing interest rates. Three distinct items, but immediately you see the connection. The incumbent party knows a stagnant economy will hurt their chances of reelection. Low interest rates might spark the economy. Will the President pressure the fed to lower interest rates?

• Connectivity is one of the answers to the "so what?" test I describe in chapter four. "So what if she has three fingers?" questions the reader. "So it ties into the rest of the plot," you can answer.

In the early draft of your story, you can answer more vaguely. "So it might not mean anything now, but it means something later. So it adds some atmosphere right now. So"—and this is the crucial part of that vague but appropriate answer—"so it gives me more to work with as I develop my story."

An example of richness in nonfiction comes from Marshall J. Cook's *Freeing Your Creativity*, a book I helped edit. Cook wrote in the first draft: "Other rewards come in due season." A touch lofty, a touch trimmable—but I asked the copy editor to not touch it when it was changed to "Other rewards may come in time." Otherwise, the grand and the evocative (bringing to mind a ripe and just harvest) would have been turned into the everyday and the pedestrian.

This is not a matter of padding. It is a matter of giving physical depth to a story, depth you can turn into storytelling depth.

So, I'm hardly eschewing the flowery. I *am* eschewing the florid.

When tight writing is distracting. A Cincinnati TV news program in the mid-1970s would present its "tease copy" (the brief "here's what's coming up" enticements) in headlinese—the abrupt, compact style of newspaper headlines. "Protesters march on capital!" "Taxes down drain!" "Newscaster uses an indefinite article in fit of eloquence!" I admit that maybe he was saving time. Two, three nanoseconds (they add up, you know). I also admit that saving time probably wasn't his intent. But the telegraphy, whatever its intent, was distracting.

Distractions are anything that take your mind off the meaning of the words and put it onto the words themselves (or, as in the above example, the *lack* of words). Distractions include:

• Unusual short words, such as new short forms like "attrit," which I discuss on page 65. They're often untested at best, and too slangishly informal at worst. Witness "rad" for "radical."

• Abbreviations. I once received a proposal for a book on business management. The book's early chapters referred frequently to the revolutionary concept of RDST management. One problem here—to save space, the author always used the abbreviation, thinking that it saved space. Four words were replaced by one acronym. Or so he thought, as ultimately the acronym was replaced in my mind by a complete sentence each time I encountered the acronym: What the heck is RDST?

RDST, so sleek and trim on the page, was a bramble in my brain, catching at me and slowing me down. It puzzled me *even though the abbreviation had been spelled out the first time it was used.* Each time I encountered it, I had to reconstruct it (or look it up). As a reader, if I'm puzzling, I'm not reading and comprehending.

Use abbreviations only if they're commonly understood (U.S.S.R., U.S.—or RDST, if your audience is business managers who use this term every day), if they can be established quickly (NAACP, RSVP), or if you can explain them fully and establish their importance early in the copy—and the explanation will stick in readers' heads. By that I mean you should carefully weigh whether the space saved will outweigh the distraction of an unusual abbreviation.

For example, I've edited the occasional article about point of view in fiction for WD magazine and books. The authors of these manuscripts often established early that "point of view" would be abbreviated POV—not a terribly unusual abbreviation, and one used often enough to be able to apply for jargon status by the turn of the century. Yet, I always asked the authors to not use the abbreviation, in part because "POV" is distracting. First, POV calls to mind a full word—"pov." A nonsense word, certainly, but a pronounceable, seemingly self-standing word nonetheless. Second, the almost gaudy all-cap abbreviation is something of a lightning rod for the eyes, drawing attention to the form of the expression and not the meaning of the expression. Therefore, it slows the reader down in its succinctness. Here, the lengthier expression is the more invisible, and therefore the more efficient.

TV is different. IRS is different.

• Unusual contractions. I would've mentioned this before, but . . . *Would've?* That's so tight, and so informal, that readers might linger over it. Or take a more common construction—"the dog's." Confusion can arise here because we don't know if we're talking about a possessive or a contraction in the first place. And, if a contraction, is it "the dog is" or "the dog has"? Often context will tell you, but suppose you read this beginning a sentence: "The dog's arriving . . ." Is "arriving" a noun, so that "dog's" is a possessive? Or is it a verb, so that "the dog's" stands for "the dog is"? Small point, but it can raise momentary confusion in the reader's mind. If there's potential for multiple interpretation, spell it out.

Certainly, not all contractions are suspect. In fact, writing "cannot" is more distracting than writing "can't," because of the formal feel and less frequent use of the former.

When tight writing becomes telegraphy. Headlinese is usually inappropriate—even in newspaper headlines. How often have you puzzled over a headline because its writer seemed to pluck six unconnected key words from the article and jam them together? I've even seen headlines that used headlinese to save space when space-saving wasn't necessary, when "Courier secures spot as United States' best" left space that could have presented the more readable "Courier secures a spot" or "his spot" or whatever. As it stands, I tend to read this headline as Mr. Courier securing the U.S.'s best friend—a dog named Spot. For that matter, perhaps the space could have been spent displaying Mr. Courier's first name, since "courier" is an occupation, and the headline could easily be misread as describing someone who had just ascended to his regal place as Slam-Bang-Best Courier, By Gosh.

A Short Summary

A general rule applies here: Don't follow writing "rules" by rote. For example, *Don't repeat a word in a sentence or more than three times in a paragraph.* Hmm. Consider, then, the real estate saw (not the "old" saw; saws are by their nature old) about what sells a house: Location! Location! Location! Or imagine Santa with but a single "Ho."

Extreme examples, but worthy. I spoke before of "I put the ball on my nose and spun it" as a dodge for repeating the word "ball" in a sentence. Or consider the danger of silly synonymity as a similar gambit. Same sentence: "I put the ball on my nose, and spun the orb." Now, that one is an entire letter shorter than the original, but it's mentally longer. "Orb" is a lame synonym, and makes you wonder if the ball and the orb are two separate objects. It's better to risk overusing a word than to risk confusion.

This problem crops up frequently in nonfiction and perhaps even more so in fiction, when writers don't want to repeat a proper name.

"I want to free the slaves," said Abraham Lincoln.

"It's unwise to declare emancipation at this point in the war, Mr. President," said Mr. Seward.

"Nonsense. Let's do it now," said the sixteenth President.

"Are you certain?"

"Yes," said the Republican from Illinois.

Sounds like we're talking about three different people: Mr. Lincoln, the sixteenth President, and the Republican from Illinois.

I even read a novel in which the author seemed afraid to use a character's name too frequently, so switched back and forth between her given name and her nickname. Every time I ran into the blander given name, I wondered, *So where did this new character come from?*

Or this oft-told advice (I told it myself earlier in this book): *Avoid weak verbs like "be."* Hmmm, again. Here, from the novel-in-progress from which "A Moment in the Sun Field" was excerpted, is a classic violation of that advice:

> "Thanks" and Bobby was slamming screen doors and pedaling off to the grocery store.

Compare that with this tighter, more active version:

> "Thanks." Bobby slammed the screen door, and pedaled off to the grocery store.

The second version is more direct, yet it's almost motionless. There's a certain telegraphy here. "Thanks." Stop. Bobby slammed the door. Stop. And pedaled off. Stop. But the first version, in its deceptively "passive" voice, has flow to it, continuing action, the sentence not bothering to stop from the time Bobby is saying "Thanks" to his hopping on his bike and scooting storeward, just as Bobby himself doesn't bother to stop. By using weak verbs, I have made a stronger sentence.

Writing must flow. It must serve not concision but other masters, primary among them the writing itself. Suppose we had applied our overactive editing ax to the words of Anton Chekhov when he said, "The art of writing is the art of abbreviation"? He might have said, "Writing is abbreviation." He might have abbreviated, "Writing: abbreviation." Or he might have telegraphed: "Write: Abbreviate."

None of which he did.

10. Putting It All Together: Writing Light

*W*e've been speaking throughout this book of writing with a light touch, of not saying what we need not say. And, ultimately, we've been speaking of stepping back, so that we the writers are turning the work over to the words.

We have another step we can take, though, to achieve graceful writing, especially in fiction, poetry and narrative nonfiction. That step involves understanding that writing is not the art of putting words to paper. It's not even the art of conceiving ideas and giving them linguistic shape within your head. Words on paper and ideas in your head are but tools you employ to accomplish the true writing.

Writing, you see, is the art of pulling triggers within the reader's brain. That's a far more abstract art than placing one word after another. I slap four letters onto a page—a *b* and an *a* and an *r* and an *n*—and I set off an image of a red building surrounded by trees and a fence and several animals. You know what a barn is, and you know that the four rounded, bending-over squiggly marks in that sequence indicate a barn. Therefore, I don't tell you things. I trigger things. I don't describe a barn. I trigger an image of a barn within your mind.

And, in doing so, I have turned the work of writing over to the words, then have subsequently turned the work of writing over to readers. The art of triggering is a crucial element of that next step toward graceful writing.

Bringing the Reader Into the Writing Process
Good writing is a matter of pulling the right triggers. Tight writing is a matter of pulling *only* the right triggers.

I do not—I cannot—create the triggers that I pull. I must depend on the triggers that you the reader supply. I can slap those four letters onto the page, *b* and *a* and *r* and *n*, but if you've never physically seen a barn, the word *or* the building, you'll never see one mentally.

Do you agree with that? You shouldn't. I *can* make you see a barn even if you haven't seen one before. I can write of the wooden sides, individual boards sometimes red, sometimes weathered to paintlessness, sometimes rotting. I can write of the air inside feeling as if captured in a greenhouse paneled in slate, of the smell of soured loam—fertilizer from the source—moist and hanging, of dust and sweet rot from the hayloft above sifting down and lingering in quiet shafts of light, feathered at the sides as they slant in from windows filmed from dirt and moisture. I can write of the concrete floor, never quite dry after animals with random bathroom habits are ushered through, after the floor has been hosed down.

If I can't trigger images directly, I must do it indirectly. I trigger images and concepts within you that, in sum, build to a feeling of what a barn might be about. The light, the dust, the smell. You might not know *barn* specifically, but you probably know *greenhouse, loam, fertilizer*. Similarly, if I can't trigger "Paris" within you directly, I can trigger it indirectly. Weather that you have experienced. A time of year you have experienced. A relationship, a type of street, a feel for how neon reflects off lighted windows.

The pinnacle of concise writing is that which allows readers to pull their own triggers. You the writer supply the facts; the readers draw their own conclusions. Fiction and narrative nonfiction should be an adventure through the wilderness, not a guided tour with stops at historical markers where the bus driver drones facts he's tired of over the PA system. In this wilderness, you have driven the trail, and you've marked it clearly; yet, readers are every bit the explorers you were. They want to discover for themselves what you have discovered in mapping out the territory before them. E.S. Creamer, a fiction editor at Putnam's, once told *Writer's Digest* readers, "Part of the joy of reading fiction is making the same creative leaps—in comprehension—that the writer makes in creation."

As example, Creamer points to one of her own short stories, "Stung," published in *Antioch Review*. She begins one section of the story this way, with no other introduction: "When I visit him in that room, its walls as white as the backs of cards well-wishers send, I wonder if his skin is milky from being so long indoors or if that, too, comes from his bones."

Is there any doubt of where "that room" is? Long stay indoors, get-well cards, and the connecting imagery of antiseptic white. Would Creamer have been wordy had she written, "When I visit him in the hospital room"? Hardly. Yet, because we understand where we are, and because Creamer isn't locked into writing "the hospital room," she can add nuance by saying "When I visit him in that room . . ." *That* room, with the implication that the viewpoint character doesn't want to be there, in *that* room.

Another example: Suppose I were to write, "Tommy read the names off the baseball card. Pete Rose, Tom Seaver, Julio Cruz. He pronounced the 'J' in 'Julio' the way he pronounced it in 'jail.' " That is nonjudgmental statement of fact. I say how he pronounced the letter; I leave it to the reader to recognize that it was the *wrong* pronunciation. On the other hand, you might argue that the fact that I brought the pronunciation up in the first place brings a certain judgment to it; if it weren't unusual, why would I have brought it up in the first place? I never explain how the character pronounces "sidewalk" or "cucumber," for instance.

Even so, these examples share one thing: The absence of the author. The reader is in "that room," seeing the cards and the white walls. The reader is beside the kid as he reads the baseball card. No author is hovering saying, "This is a hospital." No author is pointing at the kid and whispering, "He's saying it wrong," or, even worse, "He's saying it wrong because he's a naive rural kid."

Narrative glides along much faster if you don't explain everything. In fact, it can survive if you don't explain *anything*. You can communicate without explaining. You can show. You can employ context to suggest. You can let the reader put two and two together and come up with the answer, which, in fiction for instance, probably isn't "four," but "hospital." Or "elephant." Or "loyalty." Or "internal conflict."

The Power of the Specific

You'll notice that most of the elements of the $2+2=$ hospital equation—the two and its companion two—are concrete, hard-edged, definable. In a word, specific. In writing, add specific upon specific. Give the reader as much that is concrete as possible. The more concrete, the better the readers' ability to picture, to grasp. Be sure that they have not only a specific image, but also the *right* specific image.

In chapter two, I spoke of the difference between the sentences "I took my keys from a hook near the refrigerator and walked to the car" and the longer but more concrete "I snapped up my keys, hanging from a hook near the rusted Fridgidaire, and strode straight to the Mustang." Vague taking and featureless refrigerators and formless cars are mashed prose potatoes. Worse yet, reconstituted mashed prose potatoes, sticky and clinging and tasteless. Snapping up keys hanging from a hook near a brand name refrigerator and striding out to a sports car with easily pictured lines may take more words, but those words click into place in the readers' minds. The reader imagines less, has fewer possibilities to consider and select. The character is not walking to something that might be a Mustang or a Honda or a Lexus or a Yugo. He is striding to one type of car, so the reader doesn't have to spend mental nanoseconds thinking of maybe-Hondas, maybe-Lexuses or maybe-Yugos.

On the surface, this contradicts the advice to let readers do the work by not spelling everything out for them. Yet, I have not spelled *everything* out, just a few critical items. I'm not cluttering the prose with unnecessary detail — how many feet from refrigerator to car (I even skipped the door — did you miss it?), how many km/sec the character achieved at maximum speed, whether the Mustang's door was locked or unlocked. But there were things I did tell you. For instance, I told you the color of the Mustang. It was red, wasn't it? And if you hadn't pictured red, you had likely pictured some other color, some specific color I didn't have to spell out because "Mustang" has an image. It communicates its own specificity. When you think of something as distinctive as a Mustang, you quickly form a mental picture of it. Green '65 pony car. Red '68 muscle car. Black slimmed down '88 compact car. That image — whatever the image that wells up from within the reader — locks into place, says so much about what that car is that I don't have to detail. Call it essence of Mustang, different from essence of Lexus or essence of Yugo.

That leads us back to our original point, because there's no such thing as essence of *car*.

Paul Darcy Boles in his excellent *Storycrafting* refers to tapping into the "in-ness of Things":

Let's assume, for a moment, that part of your story is about the reaction of a woman to a snake.... Your task, to be performed in a minimum of words and space, is to make your reader know the essence of snakedom, the elixir of the woman. You may have read half a hundred volumes about herpetology; you may have spent an instructive summer working in the snake-house at your local zoo. But in your story what you're after is the valid center of the experience — the point, for instance, that dormant snakes smell like new-cut cucumbers; that they inspire atavistic fear, even though they're amazingly sentient, easy to handle and over-maligned. And without doing an essay on it, you will need to quickly interpret the woman's reaction to the encounter; to tell how she takes it, what she does, which will give immediate insight into the middle of her character. This is a section from a short story of mine.... Among other things, I wanted to show the impeccable calm of the woman, Phyllis, in a moment of natural crisis. The writing comes in on a slant, by indirection, embedded in the action so that inside and outside factors are working in harness. The reader sees what is going on, and feels it at the same time: "She took hold of another weed; this one deep, calling for a side twist to bring the root webs out. When she had tossed it back and was reaching for another, she saw the intruder. It was uncoiled, a flake of sun touching the triangular, turned-away head. The serrate, arid scales looked as though, if touched, they would whisper like autumn leaves. The body of the copperhead was a thick single muscle, relaxing. She sat back, hand hanging in air, then withdrew it gradually, from shade to sun."

Woman and snake are somehow together; the confrontation is mysterious and double. Here the word *description* is misleading as a cover-word for what is actually happening. The eye sees, the ear listens, the skin feels; the hand of the woman becomes the hand of the reader as it is drawn back from the shadow into the sunlight. The inwardness of snake and woman are respected and let alone to themselves. There are just sufficient words to allow the reader to participate wholly in the experience.

Boles speaks of what's internal to the snake and to the woman. Ultimately, however — and I believe Boles understood this — he speaks of the in-ness of the reader, what's internal not to things described but to things experienced by the readers. Boles is not relying on the essence of snake, but instead on the essence of human reaction to snake.

And from that sort of reliance comes a fullness that needn't be described. Boles continues, "I left out the intense fury of the late-afternoon, Fourth of July heat above the simmering Ohio River, the arcade of sun-stunned, leaf-drooping oaks in the near distance, the musky smell of the riverbank, the friable, powdery touch of the baking earth. But they are there. They're in the silence around the snake, around the woman." They're in the thick air that would support a hand already suspended by caution.

But ultimately, they are *within the reader*. Insert the snake, the sun glinting across dry scales, and the reader pulls the in-ness of the snake from the store of in-ness within the reader.

The in-ness or essence of something comes from these elements:

• What you know about it or think you know about it.
• How people react to it, consciously and subconsciously
• The image it projects.

In-ness differs from symbolism. A symbol communicates what something represents. The snake *represents* evil; the serpent, Satan. In-ness communicates what something is or appears to be, on various levels. The snake *is* frightening, *appears to be* alien.

Further Illumination

As long as we're bringing these principles into the bright light of day, let's explore how readers draw on their own in-ness and invest it into your writing with another sunshine example. In chapter two, I discussed not belaboring what the reader understands about the physical world. Let's return to that concept for a moment. What do I not have to tell you in the following sentence?

"The three of them sat hiding in the shade on the sidewalk outside Cram's Supermart, a Saturday afternoon trio of shorts and white T-shirts and sneaks."

What season is it? What's the temperature? You know the answers to those questions, because I've put you to work. Quickly, internally, you have asked yourself a couple of questions. Why was there shade? Because the sun was shining. You might get inventive here. Why was there shade? Because the moon was bright. Possible, though a bright moon would cast shadows, not shade. And why were they hiding? Because that sun was damn hot; you don't hide in the shade during a game of hide-'n-go-seek, and you don't hide in shadows to escape the sun.

We're employing the hard work done by nuance in meaning here. What's the difference in these phrases?

- The shade of the tree in the sun . . .
- The shadow of the tree in the sun . . .

The first sentence appears in a story that takes place on a day when most of us would long for an air conditioner. The second appears in a cooler setting. In the first story, we sweat in the heat. In the second, we might be trying to keep warm in the winter sun. In the first, it's late morning, noonish, early afternoon. In the second, we might be watching a cool dawn, a cooling evening of the same day. We have, in the choice of a single word, implied distinctions about the time of year, the time of day, perhaps even the setting (there's more shade in Mississippi than in Wisconsin, at least in some people's minds). So much we don't have to explain, because readers know the difference between shade and shadow. They have felt the difference between shade and shadow. We have not written, but triggered what readers know and feel.

Now, in the first example, delete the words *in the sun*. What meaning have we lost? Readers know that the sun causes shade.

So, a discussion that began with advice to include as much detail as possible has metamorphosed into one advising that you slice away detail, layer by unneeded layer. Let's revise the advice: Include as much detail *as needed*.

Pulling the right triggers also means pulling *the right number* of triggers. Overabundant detail is a trap. I once spoke to a writing group in an old school building. I told them that if I wanted, I could paint verbal pictures of the room we were in to the last detail—measure the height of the ceiling, the height of the windows, catalog which ones were open and which closed, count the chairs, quote the posters on the walls precisely, and on and on until I had digitized a photographer's image in readers' minds. But better that I take the impressionist painter's approach and speak only of ceilings so high that my voice comes back in echo that is lost in the creaking of the hardwood as I shift in my chair, in turn lost in the bleating of traffic one floor below.

As I add detail, I perfect the picture readers can form in their heads. But after a certain point, instead of bringing the image closer to readers, I draw it away from them. I say "old schoolhouse," and readers draw upon their in-ness to picture old schoolhouses they have been in. I add a few details, and I hone the image, make it more real, and communicate more specifically exactly what type of old schoolhouse I'm describing. But I add more, and I add more, and readers find it increasingly difficult to depend on their in-ness, because as I further describe something that is clearly not of their experience, the details start to fight with the details of their own memory or perceptions.

This is, of course, at odds with my points about being as concrete as possible. "Old school building" is vague, and such vagueness usurps my control over communicating what I need you the reader to know. "Old school building" to you might mean a one-room schoolhouse in a rural setting instead of the three-story late nineteenth-century stone edifice, in the middle of urban sprawl on its way to being blighted, where the meeting actually took place.

The reconciliation of the two bits of advice comes in balance, in "just enough." A few shakes of salt on the potatoes, not a couple of tablespoonfuls.

Word Weaving

Explanatory detail is a type of "too much detail." In my short story "A Moment in the Sun Field," two kids, Mike and Bobby, play a baseball game called "500" with Bobby's dad. I knew many readers might not know what 500 is. I could have settled back and given a Hoyle explanation of the rules, but the specifics of the rules weren't important; the playing of the game was. So I wove some of the rules into the playing, into the narrative. That way, the reader got a sense of the game without the story stopping: "Mike and Bobby took the field first, and Dad hit balls to them. A caught fly ball earned Bobby 100 points. A grounder played on one bounce earned Mike 75. A flubbed grounder—a two-bouncer—stole 50 points back from Mike." It's a game of points for good plays and demerits for bad—and that's all readers *need* to understand. Readers aren't going to head out and play 500 when they're done with the story; they don't need a rules manual.

A science fiction saw goes that characters in futuristic stories shouldn't pause to explain how the anti-gravity device on their personal hovercar works before they zoom off in search of plot elements, no more than a modern-day detective would explain the physics of internal combustion before roaring off to the obligatory car chase scene.

That's why you hear the advice to weave exposition (and, as important, to weave other elements, such as description and dialogue) into a story, instead of dishing it out like installments of a 101 lecture. It's the difference between weaving, with individual strands of red and blue and other colors scattered and coalescing into beautiful pattern, and quilting, with chunk of red followed by chunk of blue and the remaining other chunks. Quilts can be beautiful, but show their seams and are less homogenous than a weaving.

In a weaving, the threads coalesce to form a whole, just as tiny individual color dots coalesce in a pointillist painting (or, for that matter, in a color half-tone on the front cover of your favorite magazine) into one single, recognizable picture. In a sense, the context of the weave, the elements coming together, communicates the details sufficiently. You step back and see and understand the whole; the details—the individual threads—don't stand out, and they don't need to. You don't have to explain things when the context does the explaining for you. The context of the action of the 500 game explains the rules enough so the reader understands if not them specifically, then their intent.

Staying in Context

As important as it is to concentrate on saying what you need to say, you must also concentrate on what you *don't* need to say—what can remain unstated either because it's obvious to the readers, or because the context of your words leaves no other possibilities.

For example, suppose I write, "I left work at 5:30. When I unlocked the front door at home . . ." I don't have to say how I got home, and I don't have to say, "*Later*, when I unlocked the front door." Obviously I got home somehow. Obviously it was later.

But this works on a small scale, too. For instance, "The first time I hugged my father and was old enough to remember doing so, I was twenty-eight. He was fifty-three. He was ill and scared, and a hug was about all I could give him. After that time, before his death, I was able to watch him with my son, his only grandchild, and I knew why it took us so long. Dad smiled at Chris the way he smiled when he emerged from under a car hood . . . "

That paragraph has boundaries, walls. Think of the scene as a "room," one of the many rooms in the text. Standing in the room are me, my father, and my son. As we move through the room, through the paragraph, we encounter "I," "Dad" and "Chris." "I" is obviously me, "Dad" is obviously my father, and that leaves "Chris." No other characters have entered the "room"; Chris can be no one but my son. Process of elimination. I don't have to stick a happy-faced name-tag on that character that says, "Hi! My name is Chris, the author's son."

Again, would I have been being overly chatty had I written "Dad smiled at his grandson Chris . . ."? No. But something subtle is going on here. I am asking you to look through the viewpoint character's eyes—my eyes—so that you see the world the way the viewpoint character does. No one looks at his son and thinks, "Dad smiled at his grandson. . . ." No one labels things he or she is familiar with so blatantly. So in identifying something without externally labeling it, I have helped you ease further into the viewpoint character's mind, allowing the prose to more closely follow how the viewpoint character would view something internally.

Pulling the Trigger

To keep the "rooms" of your writing cozy and self-contained, to pull the right triggers within readers' minds, to write light, consider these suggestions.

Let your readers understand the unfamiliar by triggering the familiar. I point again to the example of the barn, to Paris. I point to the song lyric "It's a marshmallow world in the winter." The reader may not have experienced the interior of a barn, but by choosing a few apt comparisons—with imagery and figures of speech, metaphor and simile, analogy and the other tools available—you can put the reader, through accumulation, into that barn without resorting to lengthier, more detailed and more pedantic item-by-item descriptions that would be the alternative to the verbal shorthand that is the figure of speech.

The key phrase there is "through accumulation," which leads to . . .

Accumulate minor triggers to set off a major one. E.S. Creamer in her story quoted above doesn't present one commanding image to trigger "hospital" within your head. She triggers by accumulation, a detail here, a related detail there. Step back from those details and see a hospital, the same way you step back from a pointillist painting to see an image formed by the organization of individual dots.

Use one major trigger per description; others should reflect and supplement the primary trigger. I once wrote this to describe a fictional investigator, name of Ross.

> He stood now just about where he stood when he first woke me—arms dangling at his side, looking a little like my coatrack. He was slim in ways I envied, especially around the waist, and in ways I didn't, particularly around his almost fleshless face and in his legs, which looked a little like tweezers with pants on. He was my height, but his weight fell short of mine by a good thirty pounds.
>
> Ross's face had been mapped out by a cartographer who had lost his compass and his french curve. He was all straight lines, all angles, from the slashed, M-shaped hairline of his widow's peak to harsh points on his patent leather shoes. His eyebrows were bent in half, and they dangled over his eyes like the tent-shaped accent marks that hang over the vowels of some French words. His mouth was a draftsman's line with lips. I wondered if his wife had ever bruised herself while hugging his body, had ever cut herself kissing him. A perfect mouth for clipping speech.
>
> "You had better change your clothes before you hit the street, Christian," he clipped.

Well, I wrote this some time back. It's guilty of overkill. Yet, the secondary supports the primary throughout: Ross is a sharp person, figuratively and almost literally.

There is, of course, room for contrast, for the secondary that contradicts the primary—which leads to depth. Still, you should work toward a single overall impression in triggering description.

This is somewhat related to the oft-heard call against mixing metaphors: for instance, "The rock-hard hail stung like a bee." The warning against mixing metaphors doesn't result from anyone's interest in consistency as much as it does from an interest in keeping confusion (rocks? bees?) and the resulting mental distance to a minimum.

When possible, rely on a single trigger. Identify the telling detail. Is your interview subject sloppy about details. First, don't come straight out and say "Glen is sloppy about details." Show how he's sloppy. But don't catalog sloppiness. Point out that Glen dresses smartly . . . but doesn't tie his shoes.

Similarly, we might have left Ross alone after labeling him the human coatrack.

Establish artificial triggers early in the manuscript that you will pull later. In the first few paragraphs of this chapter, I said I can't create the triggers that I pull. I can, however, *plant* triggers—that is, I can *plant* seemingly meaningless triggers early in the manuscript, and pull them later.

A planted trigger is something unusual that will be easily recognized and easily connected to other elements of your story when you pull it later. A character tag is a type of trigger. An example of a tag: Sheila constantly tugs at the ends of her hair and sticks it in her ear.

When you establish these triggers early on, calling attention to them as you do so, you can swiftly reestablish characters, places, scenes later in the story. For instance, when that character sticks the ends of her hair in her ear, we know it's Sheila. We can refer to her as Sheila, but names don't often register. But we can show that this is Sheila, she of the hair in the ear from chapter two. And when we see our characters bathed again in green neon, we know we're again standing in front of the All-Night Reader's Choice Bookstore and Accessory Shop that so bathed them in chapter four.

Suggest. Hint. Imply. Yes, show us the tip of the iceberg. One ninth of the iceberg is visible; the rest is below the surface. When we look at an iceberg, we don't need to pull it from the water to examine the rest of it. We know the rest of it is there. And besides, examining the rest of it is more than superfluous. It's boring. Historical novelist Janice Young Brooks once said, "I used to get sidetracked with how people lit things—I'm part of the disposable Bic generation and don't understand flint and steel. Finally I learned to simply say, 'She lit the candle,' without worrying myself and the reader with exactly how she did it."

But go even further. Show us the silhouette of the tip of the iceberg. Show its shadow, or its outline. Better yet, don't show it at all, but show its effect: carving out its mark on yards of *Titanic* hull as sturdy as so much aluminum foil.

Ultimately, in all this discussion of triggers and 2 + 2 and silhouettes of icebergs, we have been speaking of understatement. "When you admire understatement in a story," says Paul Darcy Boles, "you are praising considerably more than good taste, which, like fastidiousness, is not a particular virtue when it stands alone; you are impressed by the author's constant consciousness of the entire world of people and things, as well as that author's ability to suggest these in microcosm without turning up the volume."

How beautiful that phrase: "suggest in microcosm without turning up the volume."

11. Tips for Trimming During Manuscript Revision

*A*s I've mentioned elsewhere in this book, I grew up in Wisconsin, in an area sculpted by glaciers whose aesthetic ran toward stone chimneys and sandstone bluffs. Killdeer and deer, scrub pine that overachieved into forest, rumors of unseen lynx. Shortly after I moved away, I camped a weekend in the Daniel Boone National Forest in Kentucky, wandering over and under natural bridges, gazing over cliffs into forest-soft, forest-deep gorges, and wondering if the people who grew up in the area realized just how beautiful it was, since they'd been born with the beauty about them.

On a trip to see family ten years later, I opened my eyes to Wisconsin, the chimneys, the bluffs, the pine. I knew someone from Kentucky was wondering if the people who grew up here realized just how beautiful it was. I knew I had an answer for that wondering Kentuckian, lucky because he was born with an eye fresh to Wisconsin, lucky because he didn't have to expatriate himself for ten years to see it for what it really was. The answer was no. I never realized.

My travels offer a lesson in manuscript revision—especially when revising for concision. When you're done with the manuscript, put it aside. Walk away from it. Not for ten years, but for a time, anyway. Allow your mind and your editorial eye, numbed by familiarity with the material, to refresh themselves, to see anew what you grew up with at the keyboard.

When you're back, apply these editing and revision suggestions:

Make that fresh return more than once. Give the final manuscript several passes, preferably over at least a couple of days. If your mind works like mine (if I can indeed call what my mind does "work"), you'll find that it's tuned to a slightly different "frequency" on each day. On one pass, it may be tuned to the tautology station, and those baby puppies will yap out loud and clear. The next pass, it may be tuned to the passivity station, call letters are-are-are-are. (Perhaps on one revision pass on this book, my mind will be tuned to the ridiculous pun station.) Each time, something else becomes apparent.

Install physical as well as temporal distance. If you handwrite your manuscripts, edit on a typewritten version. If you work on the computer, edit on hard copy (for a couple of reasons, of which more later).

Edit at a physical remove from your workspace. Read at the kitchen table, retreat to the public library, or take the manuscript along with you to lunch at your local coffee-and-pancake house.

The physical changes also freshen your editing eye. And by stepping away physically from the format and the surroundings in which you composed the prose, you have removed some of the reminders that this is Your Baby.

Keep trimming, even when you think you've taken care of a problem. The first trim usually isn't the last. For example, "The process of making the decision took weeks." Trim #1 takes it to "The decision-making process took weeks." #2: "Making the decision took weeks." #3, and best of all: "Deciding took weeks."

Closely related to this point:

When trimming, apply a general rule of proofreading and revision: Don't allow small problems to distract you from big ones. It's not unusual, for instance, for a proofreeeder to spot the obvious mispelling of "proofreader" in this sentence, but will miss the fact that "mispelling" was also misspelled. And, worse yet, the fact that the entire sentence is grammatically inconsistent (to be consistent with the infinitive "to spot," the verb "miss" should appear without "will," or should be written as "to miss").

On page 111, I point out that sometimes the word "of" signals an opportunity to shorten a phrase by using a possessive form. The sentence "We will proceed with implementation of the plan," I pointed out, could be shortened to "We will proceed with the plan's implementation." But, because of another problem discussed in detail on page 113, the sentence can be further shortened to "We will implement the plan." And so we've been very busy with our nips and tucks, completely oblivious to the fact that the sentence, oh so shortened and concise, is still pretty stiff. Maybe you could communicate the same thought with a simple "Let's do it."

Review the manuscript for large problems first, and go for the smaller stuff later. On each of the multiple passes described in the first point, assign yourself a primary goal. On the first pass, concentrate on the flow of the manuscript, whether material is pertinent, whether it makes sense. Is it too long? Does it *feel* too long? Does it flow evenly and at an appropriate pace, or do you run into slow spots?

Don't ignore smaller issues as you read, but don't let them distract you from getting an overall sense of whether your writing accomplishes what you want it to. Circle or flag, say, passive phrasings you spot, but don't correct them now. Keep your mind tuned to one station before moving on to the next.

On succeeding passes, watch for smaller problems—an unneeded aside, too many examples, a throat-clearing transition—and then smaller problems still—a circuitous phrasing, a redundancy, an "of" that can go. There's no sense spending time changing passive phrasings to the active in a paragraph you end up cutting later on.

Don't consign your concision review to the final draft. As I've advised before, review what you've written at the end of every writing session. If you spot redundancies and such, attack them.

But don't fixate on them. Use this review as an opportunity to spot not just what you've done wrong, but also what you've done right. This will give you energy and confidence that will make starting your next writing session all the easier.

If you prefer, handle this as I've suggested before, as a prewriting review instead of a postwriting review; read the previous day's work before you start your next writing session.

Don't trim blindly. No knee-jerk chopping, please. You must look at the repetitious material in context. For example, as discussed in "How Tight Is Too Tight?" on page 145, redundancy can be a tool for establishing clarity, pace and rhythm. So deleting a redundancy might solve one problem—wordy repetition—while creating another—arrhythmic, less-clear prose. Take, for instance, a common redundant conjunction, "and also." Since they're synonymous, there's no point in pairing the words. Next up: "and also, too." But, in this case, there *is* a point to pairing the words, though it has little to do with their meaning. To examine what I mean, consider this sentence:

> I stood at the doorstep and surveyed the freshly mown grass, the neat sidewalk, the trees in bloom, and also my smashed car in the driveway.

Consider it in its trimmed version:

> I stood at the doorstep and surveyed the freshly mown grass, the neat sidewalk, the trees in bloom, and my smashed car in the driveway.

In the first version, "and also" is a pacing tool, adding a pause, a hesitation that isolates the smashed car from everything else in the front yard that is as it should be. It helps the reader understand the contrast. I've seen numerous occasions where "and also" provided similar rhythm to a sentence. So, forgive "and also"? No. It's still distractingly redundant. In this case, use the phrase "as well as." Not as trim as "and," but useful.

A long example to make an important point I've made before but will reiterate: Repetition doesn't necessarily signal only verbosity. It can signal the need for deeper work on the manuscript. Ask yourself if the redundancy serves a function beyond meaning. And if it does, how else can you perform that function with words that work, or, at the very least, don't distract?

If you trim blindly, you miss the opportunity to improve the prose with other writing techniques.

If you work on a word processor, perform significant after-the-first-draft trimming on a paper copy of your manuscript, not on the screen. Or, if you do work on the screen, keep an archive copy of the original draft somewhere on disk. How frustrating to chop that well-worded but unneeded paragraph, only to decide later that it would make an interesting sidebar or the core of an entirely different article, but you've bulk-deleted it into word-processing limbo. If you have a computer copy of the original draft, or if you've hand-edited on paper, you can recover or reconstruct your deletion.

If you're simply eliminating redundancies and such, working on the screen is fine, especially if you're using the computer's search function to seek pet wordiness (such as I describe on page 102). But for more substantive examinations, I find that working with words on paper gives me a better feel for them. On paper, they are closer physically and in spirit to their eventual printed form.

Use the dictionary and the style manuals frequently. And please stay away from computer spellcheck programs that do nothing more than check spellings. These are called "dictionary" programs, and I wonder sometimes if there was more cynicism than laziness in labeling them so. A dictionary is so much more than a list of proper spellings. Consult the dictionary for word meanings, too. Most "dictionary" programs don't supply those. Sure, spellchecks have their place. They can tell you that you don't really mean to write "comradery." You mean "camaraderie." But, as I've pointed out before, maybe once you look it up in a good wordbook that explains word origins and implications, you'll find that you really meant to write "friendship" in the first place.

Get your hands dirty as you look up these words. Don't distance yourself from them with computer technology that robs you of the opportunity to learn more about them.

Also, remember the copy editor's credo: If you're unsure about a word, look it up. If you're absolutely certain about it, look it up.

Save deleted material in some form, for the reasons mentioned above. But there's another reason to save deletions, especially long ones. In *Getting the Words Right*, Theodore Cheney tells of how difficult it is to admit that entire chapters might be superfluous, and how painful it is to delete those chapters when they are. He stores long deletions in a notebook labeled "For possible inclusion." He says, "I've found this a comforting bit of self-deception. By having a definite place to keep my verbal deadweight, a sort of organized attic, I don't mind deleting it."

Make certain that you follow through on any deletions. Suppose I had decided that my reference to the Svoboda Principles in the above paragraph was superfluous and deleted it? Confused? You've never heard of the Svoboda Principles until now, have you? That's because I referred to them in an early draft of this book, and deleted them. (Actually, I made him up for the purposes of this illustration, but you get the point.) Svoboda disappears once, I'd better make

sure he disappears throughout the manuscript—or is properly introduced at the appropriate time. When you make a major deletion, such
as clipping out a source, eliminating a character or deleting a scene,
scan the rest of the manuscript for subsequent references.

If you're working on a word processor, search the rest of the
manuscript for a key word, such as "Svoboda." Better yet, search
with a couple of key words; search for "principle," in case you later
wrote about the principles Svoboda espoused without repeating his
name.

Go back to your notes and look up the interview with Svoboda.
What else did the interview touch on? Where else might you have
introduced those principles? Check those parts of the manuscript.

Jot yourself a note about major sections you've deleted; refer to
the note before you review the final draft of your manuscript so
you'll be more attuned to spotting references you might have missed.

**Always review your manuscript in its entirety, start to finish,
after substantive cutting.** Mr. Svoboda may have served more than
one function in the manuscript. Yes, he supplied information you
decided wasn't crucial to the manuscript. But perhaps you also used
his comments to swing a transition. Perhaps the paragraphs you
devoted to him balanced the manuscript as a whole. A start-to-finish
read will help you spot any choppiness, imbalances or other problems
introduced by your concision work.

Again, to increase your objectivity, let some time pass before
doing this start-to-finish review.

Retype troublesome parts. That's a moot point if you still work on
a typewriter—you're likely to retype *everything*, and that's good, for
reasons I'll detail in a moment. But if you word-processing writers
encounter a difficult passage, run it through the brain and the keyboard again, and let that brain processor work on the problems as
you retype. In fact, as I hinted at a moment ago, consider retyping
the entire manuscript, especially when rewriting or revising heavily.
As I've noted elsewhere, that suggestion is blasphemy to the ears
of the word-processing faithful. But retyping allows you to further
sift the words, the sentences, the whole manuscript, through your
mind and through your fingers. Follow the words as you revise.
Weigh them and their relationship to the other words. Do they make
sense? Are they necessary? Do they flow?

Piecemeal tinkering gives you a good view of some of the trees in your manuscript, and allows you to add and subtract and grow a fine lot of trees. But you must stroll through the forest when rewriting. You must close your eyes and sense the fullness of the woods, the smells of the trees and the sounds of the birds and the coolness of the air. Retyping from scratch gives you that perspective.

Rereading the manuscript allows some of that perspective, but from the reader's point of view: You see the results. Retyping from scratch gives you the writer's point of view, one aided—and clarified—by the excitement of the hands-on element of creation.

Retyping also allows you to fully process changes. Suppose you type, "A person makes the changes required of him." If you want to remove the sex-specific references (it's a generic person, a generic him), you might want to change singular "him" to plural "them." That will require additional change in the sentence: "a person" becomes "people," and with a few keystrokes on the word processor, person multiplies into people, him multiplies into them. And you have a very nice sentence: "People makes the changes required of them." You have processed individual elements of the sentence, letting the agreement change in the verb slip by. But if you were to change the sentence by retyping it from scratch, you would address the verb agreement—unconsciously—as you put the words to paper.

Escape to Wisconsin. It's a beautiful place, now that I've *seen* it.

12. Shave and a Haircut and a Few Bits

Sometimes trimming is like shaving. A few touches of the razor to the face or leg to take care of a millimeter's worth of stubble makes you look oh so much better.

Strop your razor; we're about to do some shaving. With a flick of the editing wrist, we are going to lop off a letter here, maybe a couple more there. All in all, a series of nips and tucks that seem cosmetic but aren't. Cuts that add even a bit of readability to your writing are more than cosmetic. Cuts that increase your awareness of even minute opportunities for streamlining your prose are more than cosmetic.

Use contractions as appropriate. Contractions lend an informal tone and are fairly invisible. "Can't" instead of "cannot," "won't" instead of "will not," "I'll" instead of "I will." (How about a *formal* contraction, though? "Shan't.")

Avoid contractions, however, if:

• The tone of the manuscript is formal.
• You use distractingly clumsy or little-used contractions: "God'll get you for that." "I should've known."

Also beware "hidden wordiness" contractions can lead to. For instance, the sentence "I've got a book" contains the not only wordy but also sloppy construction "have got." Instead: "I have a book."

In order to tighten sentences, get rid of "in order."

Wordy: In order to get the job done, keep at it.
Better: To get the job done, keep at it.

Avoid "nonquotational" quotes, unless you "really" need them.
Swatting a couple of gnatty quote marks out of your copy isn't going
to save much space, but it will speed readers along, because they
won't pause at the word you bestowed importance upon with your
quotation marks. In a sentence above, the quote marks around "nonquotational" are needed, in that I want to signal that, yeah, I know,
it's not a real word. But those around "really" add nothing—except
additional attention from the reader. (Which brings up the point:
Reconsider using any words that you must set off with quotation
marks. Is there a more efficient and less distracting way to make
your point?)

If appropriate, address the reader in the second person. Doing
so reduces distance between writer and reader, and it's a touch
shorter.

> *Wordy:* Using the second person will benefit the writer.
> *With greater impact:* Using the second person will benefit you.

Drop the "and" before the final item in a series. Every once in a
while, anyway, and only for effect.
Example: We stocked up on provisions: food, water, fuel.
This lends a compactness, a matter-of-factness, to the prose, and
tightens the relationship of the items in the series, lined up so close
together as they are. It also removes an arrhythmic element when
you're establishing rhythm in a series. Notice the rhythmic differences in the following:

> The good, the bad and the ugly.
> The good, the bad, the ugly.

Don't number what the reader can count. "Training a dog and
training a cat are *two* completely different challenges," or "Elm, oak
and maple are *three* examples of trees." Or an odd variant popular in
the sports world, "I'm referring to one Bo Jackson." I concede that
the phrase is a legitimate device that confers tribute upon Mr.
Jackson. In fact, saying "one Bo Jackson" is better than resorting to
clichés like "the one and only Bo Jackson." Yet, when I hear this
several times in a sportscast, I want to snap back, "I'm glad we're
not talking about two Bo Jacksons."

Similarly, don't number what you don't have to. For example, this phrase: "twenty-eight one-hundredths of a second." As opposed to twenty-eight *two*-hundredths? "Twenty-eight hundredths" will do.

Beware the "re-" redundancy. I heard a politician speaking of "re-righting the economy" when we would have been happy if it were simply "righted." Beware the pesky "re-" prefix; it can sneak in quietly. "Let's revisit that situation." Have we visited it in the first place?

Drop understood phrases, as in the following examples:

It was doubtful whether or not he would participate.
It was doubtful whether he would participate.

The building that is on your left is City Hall.
The building on your left is City Hall.

Snip snip the syllables in the following words:

Trimmable: Most importantly, be concise.
Trimmed: Most important, be concise.

Trimmable: We looked down upon the valley.
Trimmed: We looked down on the valley.

Beware the archaic. Oftentimes, you can get away with words like "whilst." Often it's better to go with "while." A fellow editor once told me (I wish I had said it), "You can't have archaic and edit, too."

So, a "daemon" should be a "demon"; an "encyclopaedia" is big enough as it is, so make it "encyclopedia"; and although "archaeological" has the appropriate taste of antiquity to it, we should use modern "archeological" methods.

A "shoppe" is a "shop" (unless it's very "olde").

And, finally, chop with the "ax," sharper than the "axe."

Don't go overboard in indicating times. This has a variety of implications. "My husband was born in 1955 A.D." "The sun comes up at 6:00 A.M. in the morning." "The time is 7:55 o'clock." And, finally, something like "5:00" can become "5" when it's clear that the "5" refers to time: "Meet me at 5," or "I got up at 5 A.M."

Move toward concision, not towards it. Similarly, lop off the "s" in such words as "backwards," "forwards," "upwards" and "afterwards."

Beware the tiny but prevalent "it."
"It so happens that . . ."
"It came to pass that . . ."
"It says in today's paper . . ."
What is this all-speaking but unseen "it"? Probably being spoken by the all-speaking but unseen "they" (as in, "*They* say not to use 'it.' "). The first two phrases quoted above can be eliminated. The third can be reworded to say, "Today's paper says . . ."

Use "there" only to point at something. First, there's the problem of . . . the first problem comes from "there" simply getting in the way. "There is a plan on the table." Better is "A plan is on the table." Second is the redundancy created by the implications of what "there" often refers to. Physical things have a certain "thereness" about them." We call them physical because they are, well, "there." So we can eliminate "there" in constructions like "The bench was *there* in the park." (The same goes for sentences like "The bench was *situated* in the park" or "The bench was *located* in the park.") *Unless* the "there" clarifies something — as opposed to the bench being *here* in the park, *way over there* in the park, or whatever.

Don't include "etc." and "and so on" in a list kicked off by the word "include." For example, "The seasons include summer and fall." "Include" signals that the list that follows might be partial. But if you were to say, "The seasons are summer and fall, etc.," the "etc." is doing its work of explaining that the list continues, because that sentence has no such clue.

Just skip the facts, ma'am.

Wordy: I'm amazed by the fact that you took the last cookie.
Better: I'm amazed that you took the last cookie.

Use "use" cautiously. Sometimes the fact that you are using something is understood. For example:

> *Wordy:* For this exam, you need to use a pencil.
> *Better:* For this exam, you need a pencil.

and:

> *Wordy:* A sharp knife is dangerous to use.
> *Better:* A sharp knife is dangerous.

Beware the potential wordiness of informality and colloquialisms.

> *Wordy:* Watch out for wordiness.
> *Better:* Beware wordiness.

As always, let context and communication decide the proper words. For instance, there's a difference between being wary of something and watching out for something; I can watch out for Christmas sales, which doesn't mean I'm wary of them.

"As" — you don't like it. "As" can signal little problems. For instance, change "as of late" to "lately." Other examples: Change "He hasn't responded as of yet" to "He hasn't responded yet." Worse yet is something like, "He hasn't responded as of now." (Also consider if you need "yet" in these sentences. "He hasn't responded" might communicate just as much as "He hasn't responded yet," though the latter communicates that he likely will respond eventually.)

On another matter, watch where "as" itself can be excised. "She was labeled as a crank" can be pared to "She was labeled a crank."

Don't show the way. Show how. For example, change "That's the way to do it" to "That's how to do it."

How come you ask "how come?"? Why not ask why?

And miscellaneous other nips and tucks:

- Change "approximately the same length" to "about as long" (these two are hardly approximately the same length).
- Change "point of view" to "view" (or "opinion," if appropriate).
- Change "currently" to "now."
- Phrases like "a small number of people" can be changed to "a few people." Better yet, be specific: "Three people."
- "Appear on the scene" is long; "arrive" is better.
- Change "no matter what the circumstances" to "no matter the circumstances."
- Change "in back of" to "behind" and "in front of" to "before."

Bibliography and Sources

*T*hese books and publications will help you tighten your work. Some are, I concede, from the publisher of *this* book, the publisher I work for. I mention them not because the sellers sign my paychecks or even because I edited them (in most cases, I didn't), but because I learned from them.

Books

Currently out of print but well worth some hunting through libraries and used bookstores is *Storycrafting*, by Paul Darcy Boles. Originally published by Writer's Digest Books, it is the finest discussion of efficient internal fiction mechanics I've seen.

I've spent quite a bit of space in this book advising you to not put to paper what is already understood, so I won't tell you to study *The Elements of Style*, by William Strunk and E.B. White. You're a writer and you already understood that, right?

William Lutz's *Doublespeak* has double edges; it is both entertaining and frightening. Lutz chairs the Committee on Public Doublespeak of the National Council of Teachers of English, and edits the *Quarterly Review of Doublespeak* (of which, more later). Doublespeak is evasive, often circuitous, language: "light" meals and beer in advertising instead of diet meals and beer as a "light" example; "radiation enhancement device" instead of neutron bomb as the second edge. The book's intention is primarily to illuminate evasion and the art of misleading—often motivated by cynicism—but its lessons about wordiness are clear. Make procurement actions from HarperPerennial (a division of HarperCollinsPublishers, sic—aren't you grateful that publishers are serving concision by eliminating spaces?).

Getting the Words Right, by Theodore Cheney, covers revision as its central focus — and discusses "revision by reduction" in the first of the book's three sections. Available from Writer's Digest Books.

Guide to Concise Writing: The Source for Clear, Effective Writing is a marvelous reference work written by Robert Hartwell Fiske and published by Webster's New World (a division of Simon & Schuster). Most of its many pages are dedicated to a "Dictionary of Concision," starting with "abolish altogether" (which Fiske tells us to replace with "abolish" or "eliminate") and finishing with "zoological garden," which Fiske slices down to the more familiar and harder-working "zoo."

From Twain Productions is *Write Smarter, Not Harder*, by Joe Floren. It's not as effective as it might be in giving you ways of tackling wordiness, but the book's early chapters engagingly make you aware of the presence of wordiness and its effects, especially in business communications.

Richard Lederer is a fun and instructive observer of the language; look up his *Get Thee to a Punnery* or *Anguished English* (Pocket Books), or any of his other titles.

With grace and style, the late Robert Claiborne discusses the roots of English in *Our Marvelous Native Tongue*, still available in both hardcover from Times Books and paperback from Random House. Learn why we speak and write the way we do, and give yourself greater control over the language and greater freedom in its use. Best of all, Claiborne keeps his native tongue firmly in his cheek when appropriate, instructing and informing with wit and as much love for this majestic language as you and I have. (Of secondary interest is the less detailed *The Mother Tongue: English and How It Got That Way*, by Bill Bryson, from Morrow in hardcover and Avon in paper. *The Story of English*, written by Robert McCrum, William Cran, and Robert MacNeil and published by Viking in hardcover and Penguin in paper, is a companion to a PBS series by the same name. There are other books on the topic; start with Claiborne.)

Fascinating as much for its ambitious quest as for its instruction is E.W. Kellogg's *To Be or Not*, an anthology of essays. Kellogg and friends espouse *never* using forms of the verb "to be" (except in book titles, apparently). Probably not in your bookstore, so write the publisher, the International Society of General Semantics, P.O. Box 728, Concord, California 94522.

Out of print, but worth a check at the library card catalog is Kit Reed's *Revision*, which offers tips for trimming fiction amidst its

wealth of fiction-revision tips. Reed's *Mastering Fiction Writing* (Writer's Digest Books) also includes advice for achieving clarity of voice and style in fiction.

Donna Levin's *Get That Novel Started!* (Writer's Digest Books) also outlines a number of ways to *keep that novel going* — and in doing so lists fiction digressions and redundancies that can clog up your tale.

Make Your Words Work actually makes *you* work — at writing with power and impact. Author Gary Provost offers hundreds of tips for keeping your nonfiction or fiction sharp and streamlined. Writer's Digest Books, once more.

And while we're talking about that publisher that I have a fair bit of familiarity with, William Noble's *28 Writing Blunders (and How to Avoid Them)* offers marvelous lessons in how to break the writing rules to good effect.

Books by other language observers can broaden your knowledge of and control over the language. James J. Kilpatrick's *The Art of Writing* (Andrews and McMeel) is useful. William Safire has an intelligent and witty view of the language; any of his books will entertain and benefit you.

Publications

These periodicals aid in your vigilance against redundancies and language misuse, both classic and faddish:

The National Council of Teachers of English publishes the excellent *Quarterly Review of Doublespeak* (1111 Kenyon Road, Urbana, Illinois 61801). This newsletter collects examples of current verbal obsfucation, as well as articles about the topic. These folks also make annual awards to the worst verbal offenders, as well as to those who further clarity in writing.

Keeping an *Editorial Eye* out for things is a newsletter aimed at editors but equally useful to writers. *Editorial Eye* takes language misuse to task, and tells you how to correct problems. Its book reviews are also interesting. (Editorial Experts, Inc., 66 Canal Center Plaza, Suite 200, Alexandria, Virginia 22314)

Writer's Digest publishes the occasional article on language use in addition to its writing-technique articles. Of special interest is the "Grammar Grappler" column written by Richard Lederer, the author of *Anguished English*, mentioned above. (1507 Dana Avenue, Cincinnati, Ohio 45207)

For the business communicator, *Communications Briefings* includes the occasional concision tip in its range of coverage—and is in itself a study in tight presentation of material. Expensive, but worth a look. (700 Black Horse Pike, Suite 110, Blackwood, New Jersey 08012)

Appendix:
A Baedeker of the Redundant

*T*his list of redundant phrases is but partial; additions must made before it's "fully comprehensive." I welcome "more additions" to the list.

abandoned derelict
absolute dogma/fact/
    truth
absolutely certain/
    sure
absolutely conclusive
absolutely essential/
    indispensable/
    necessary
actual fact/truth
added bonus
additional accessory
add together
add up
adequate enough
admit to
advance ahead/
    forward/on/up
advance forecast/
    prediction
advance notice/
    warning
advance plan/
    preparation
advance registration

advance reservation
again reiterate
all complete/done
all-time record
alongside of
already existing
alternative choice
A.M. in the morning
annual birthday
another additional
another alternative
appointed as
appreciate in value
assemble together
as yet (unless it
    begins a sentence)
attach together
auction sale
audible to the ear

baby kid/kitten/
    puppy/etc.
balance out
bald-headed

basic fundamental/
    principle
blended together
botch up
bouquet of flowers
brief moment
build up
but however

cancel out
cash money
chowder soup
clearly apparent
close down
close proximity
coequal
collect together
combined together
completely engulf
completely full
completely ignore
condense down
confess to
connected together
consensus of opinion

continue on
continues to remain
contributing factor
correlated together
could possibly/
    potentially
crazy maniac
currently pending
current news
current record

daily journal
deadly killer
deliberate lie
direct confrontation
disappear from sight
drop down

Easter Sunday
empty space
empty vacuum
end result
equally as
equal to one another
erode away
established fact
exact match
exact same
excess waste
extra bonus

fall down
false pretenses
fatal suicide
few in number
fiction novel
filled to the brim
fill up
first began/created/

invented/
    originated
first established/
    discovered/
    uncovered
first introduced/
    revealed/unveiled
floral bouquet
follows behind
foot pedal
forecast the future
foreign imports
foresee the future
forward progress
free gift
freeze up
French cuisine
from whence
future hope
future plan
future prospect
future site

gambling casino
gather together
general public
genuine sincerity

head up
hope for the future
hurry up

identical match
immediately
    adjoining
I myself
inadvertent oversight
inconsequential
    drivel
increasingly more
initial introduction

interpret to mean
in the time since
intimately familiar
I personally

joint agreement/
    cooperation/co-
    sponsorship
join together
just exactly
just recently

kneel down
knots per hour
known fact

large-sized
later on
left-hand side
lend out
level to the
    ground (v.)
lift up
link together
little bit
local neighbors
located right (on the
    spot)
lose out on

major breakthrough
many in number
map out
mass exodus
mass extinction
may or may not
may possibly
maximum limit
meaningless
    gibberish

meet together
melt down
mental telepathy
merge into one
merge together
meshed together
might or might not
might possibly/
    potentially
mingle together
minute detail
mix together
more preferable
most but not all
mull over (worse yet:
    mull over in your
    mind)
mutual agreement/
    communication/
    consent/
    cooperation/
    friendship

name as
native habitat
natural instinct
necessary
    prerequisite/
    requirement/
    requisite
neither one
never before
never ever
new baby
new beginning
new creation/
    discovery/
    innovation/
    invention
new record

new recruit
noontime
now current
now pending

old adage/cliché/
    maxim/proverb/
    saw/saying
old antique
old relic
open up
optional accessory
orbiting satellite
originally began/
    created/
    discovered/
    established/
    founded
originally revealed/
    unveiled
other alternative

pack together
pair of twins
pare down
past accomplishment/
    achievement/deed/
    experience/
    history/
    performance/
    precedence/record
pay out
penetrate into
perfect Utopia
person who
physically located
place where
plan ahead
plan of action
plan out

plummet down
plunge down
P.M. in the afternoon/
    in the evening/at
    night
popular consensus
positive assurance
possible candidate/
    prospect
possibly may/might
potential candidate/
    prospect
potentially may/
    might
pour down
predict the future
preliminary draft
prepare before/in
    advance
preplan
present incumbent
previous history
previously existing
prior approval/
    blessing/consent
proceed ahead/
    forward/on
protrude out
pure unadulterated

quickly expedite
quickly flee

radiate out
raining outside
raise up
raze to the ground
reason is because
reason why
recall back

receive back
recoil back
recorded history
recur again
reduce down
refer back
reflect back
regular routine
reiterate again
relate back
relic of the past
remaining remnant/
  vestige
remand back
remit back
repay back
repeat over
reply back
report back
residual trace
respond back
restore back
resume again
retreat back
return back
revert back
right-hand side
rise up
root cause
rough sketch
routine procedure

Sahara Desert
same identical
same precise
seek out
separate entity/
  individual
separate out
serious crisis

serve up
share together
single solitary
sink down
skilled craftsman/
  woman
skip over
skirt around
slight trace
small-sized
small smidgeon/trace
snowing outside
so consequently/
  therefore
spin in circles
springtime
spur on
stack together
stand up
starve to death
steam calliope
strangle to death
summertime
sum total
swallow down
switchblade knife
switch over

talking out loud
temporary reprieve
temporary stopgap
tense up
Thanksgiving
  Thursday
thieves' argot
time when
tiny bit
tiny particle
total up
totally devoted

trace amount
true facts

ultimate limit
unexpected surprise
unintentional
  mistake
unite together
unneeded verbiage
up for sale
up 'til/until

valuable asset
vantage point
verbal discussion
violent explosion
visible to the eye
vital necessity
volley back and forth

wait around
weather conditions
weave together
weld together
whether or not
while at the same
  time/while
  simultaneously
whittle down
wink an eye
wintertime
written down

x-ray photograph

young child/foal/kid/
  kitten/lad/puppy/
  etc.

zoom up

Apologia

Somewhere, somewhere, somewhere in this book is a redundancy, an unneeded word or phrase, a spot of self-indulgence, and perhaps even a horde or two of each. You'll find them. And when you write to me about them % Writer's Digest Books, 1507 Dana Avenue, Cincinnati, OH 45207, I'll try to be cheerful about being found out, and make corrections in upcoming editions. (We may even put a banner on the cover proclaiming, as did a revised edition of the best-selling *And the Band Played On*: "Including a new update.")

But when you write to me, I'll affect the pose used by cats when they sprawl on a slippery floor—even if I'm flat on my face, I'll look at your letter and say, "I meant to do that." And most times, I'll actually mean it. I purposely used "somewhere" three times in the first sentence of this apologia. And I realize the self-indulgent unnecessity of "a horde or two," but I put it to paper anyway. And I know that "unnecessity" is barely a word, if at all. But, hey, you know what I meant, and I'm having fun, and perhaps so are you.

Now that you've completed *Write Tight*, I can afford a confession. You've just read a book on concision by a man who has used, almost proudly, defiantly, most unconcisely, the phrase "hot water heater" throughout his life, in speech and in print. "But it's redundant," argue the arguers. "It says nothing more than 'water heater' does." Well, I contend that even if the machine is filled with hot water, when the heating element fires up to make water hotter—to heat it—it makes already hot water even hotter. So you can, therefore, have a hot water heater. On the other hand, the phrase "hottest water heater" doesn't work.

The point is that like many things in our imprecise lives, concision is a relative, individual thing. I won't belabor the points I made in my chapter on how tight is too tight, except to stress that English was born, it seems, to be played with. We can afford to be playful. And English is a language that we allow to breathe. All languages are like that, I suppose; English is the only one I can comment on with any authority. English breathes, without threat of bursting linguistic seams, or of our etymological belts coming undone and leaving our pants at our ankles.

In that spirit, I welcome your comment, your suggestions and your corrections, if you as enthusiastically welcome my right to differ. Because it is in the differing that style resides and that the language thrives.

Index

Other Books of Interest

General Writing Books
Beginning Writer's Answer Book, edited by Kirk Polking (paper) $13.95
Beginnings, Middles and Ends by Nancy Kress $13.95
Dare to Be a Great Writer, by Leonard Bishop (paper) $14.95
Discovering the Writer Within, by Bruce Ballenger & Barry Lane $17.95
Freeing Your Creativity, by Marshall Cook $17.95
Getting the Words Right: How to Rewrite, Edit and Revise, by Theodore A. Rees Cheney (paper) $12.95
How to Write a Book Proposal, by Michael Larsen (paper) $11.95
How to Write Fast While Writing Well, by David Fryxell $17.95
How to Write with the Skill of a Master and the Genius of a Child, by Marshall J. Cook $18.95
Just Open a Vein, edited by William Brohaugh $6.99
Knowing Where to Look: The Ultimate Guide to Research, by Lois Horowitz (paper) $18.95
Make Your Words Work, by Gary Provost $17.95
On Being a Writer, edited by Bill Strickland (paper) $16.95
Pinckert's Practical Grammar, by Robert C. Pinckert (paper) $11.95
Shift Your Writing Career into High Gear by Gene Perret $16.95
The 30-Minute Writer: How to Write and Sell Short Pieces by Connie Emerson $17.95
12 Keys to Writing Books That Sell, by Kathleen Krull (paper) $12.95
The 28 Biggest Writing Blunders, by William Noble $12.95
The 29 Most Common Writing Mistakes & How to Avoid Them, by Judy Delton (paper) $9.95
The Wordwatcher's Guide to Good Writing & Grammar, by Morton S. Freeman (paper) $15.95
Word Processing Secrets for Writers, by Michael A. Banks & Ansen Dibell (paper) $14.95
The Writer's Book of Checklists, by Scott Edelstein $16.95
The Writer's Digest Guide to Manuscript Formats, by Buchman & Groves $18.95
The Writer's Essential Desk Reference, edited by Glenda Neff $19.95

Nonfiction Writing
The Complete Guide to Writing Biographies, by Ted Schwarz $6.99
How to Do Leaflets, Newsletters, & Newspapers, by Nancy Brigham (paper) $14.95
How to Write Irresistible Query Letters, by Lisa Collier Cool (paper) $10.95
The Writer's Complete Guide to Conducting Interviews by Michael Schumacher $14.95
The Writer's Digest Handbook of Magazine Article Writing, edited by Jean M. Fredette (paper) $11.95
Writing Articles From the Heart: How to Write & Sell Your Life Experiences by Marjorie Holmes $16.95

Fiction Writing
The Art & Craft of Novel Writing, by Oakley Hall $17.95
Best Stories from New Writers, edited by Linda Sanders $5.99

Characters & Viewpoint, by Orson Scott Card $13.95
The Complete Guide to Writing Fiction, by Barnaby Conrad $18.95
Creating Characters: How to Build Story People, by Dwight V. Swain $16.95
Creating Short Fiction, by Damon Knight (paper) $11.95
Dialogue, by Lewis Turco $13.95
The Fiction Writer's Silent Partner, by Martin Roth $19.95
Get That Novel Started! (And Keep Going 'Til You Finish), by Donna Levin $17.95
Handbook of Short Story Writing: Vol. I, by Dickson and Smythe (paper) $12.95
Handbook of Short Story Writing: Vol. II, edited by Jean Fredette (paper) $12.95
How to Write & Sell Your First Novel, by Collier & Leighton (paper) $12.95
Manuscript Submission, by Scott Edelstein $13.95
Mastering Fiction Writing, by Kit Reed $18.95
Plot, by Ansen Dibell $13.95
Practical Tips for Writing Popular Fiction, by Robyn Carr $17.95
Scene and Structure by Jack Bickham $14.95
Spider Spin Me a Web: Lawrence Block on Writing Fiction, by Lawrence Block $16.95
Theme & Strategy, by Ronald B. Tobias $13.95
The 38 Most Common Writing Mistakes, by Jack M. Bickham $12.95
Writer's Digest Handbook of Novel Writing, $18.95
Writing the Novel: From Plot to Print, by Lawrence Block (paper) $11.95

The Writing Business
A Beginner's Guide to Getting Published, edited by Kirk Polking (paper) $11.95
Business & Legal Forms for Authors & Self-Publishers, by Tad Crawford (paper) $4.99
The Complete Guide to Self-Publishing, by Tom & Marilyn Ross (paper) $18.95
How to Write with a Collaborator, by Hal Bennett with Michael Larsen $1.00
How You Can Make $25,000 a Year Writing, by Nancy Edmonds Hanson (paper) $14.95
This Business of Writing, by Gregg Levoy $19.95
Writer's Guide to Self-Promotion & Publicity, by Elane Feldman $16.95
Writing A to Z, edited by Kirk Polking $24.95

To order directly from the publisher, include $3.00 postage and handling for 1 book and $1.00 for each additional book. Allow 30 days for delivery.

Writer's Digest Books
1507 Dana Avenue, Cincinnati, Ohio 45207
Credit card orders call TOLL-FREE
1-800-289-0963
Stock is limited on some titles; prices subject to change without notice.

Write to this same address for information on *Writer's Digest* magazine, *Story* magazine, Writer's Digest Book Club, Writer's Digest School, and Writer's Digest Criticism Service.